D1316032

LOGIC

A Guided Introduction

Contents

CHAPTER 1
Recognizing and Analyzing Arguments

Chapter 1

Recognizing and Analyzing Arguments

This is a book about logic. **Logic** is the study of arguments. When we use the term "arguments" here, we aren't talking about quarreling, debate, or the power of persuasion. Those are fine things to study, but they aren't what we are concerned with in this book. An **argument** is a set of ideas that can be divided into premises and a conclusion. The **premises** are the parts of an argument that are supposed to be evidence for or reasons to believe the conclusion. And, the **conclusion** is the idea or claim inferred from the premises. Here's a quick example.

> Premise 1: The Bellagio Hotel and Casino has been robbed.
> Premise 2: Danny Ocean, a known thief was seen lurking around the Bellagio in the days prior to the heist.
> Premise 3: Since the robbery, Danny Ocean and his pals have been seen spending an inordinate amount of cash.
> Premise 4: Security cameras show that the thief seems to match Danny Ocean's height and weight *exactly*.
> *Therefore*,
> Conclusion: Danny Ocean robbed the Bellagio Hotel and Casino.

If you believe that premises 1 – 4 are true, it might be natural (and perhaps *rational*) to also believe that the conclusion is true as well. Likewise, premises 1 – 4 certainly seem to serve as evidence for (but not *proof* of!) the conclusion. If the police found out that the premises of this argument are true, they'd certainly want to sit down and have a chat with Mr. Ocean.

Here's another example.

> Premise 1: If it's wrong for Jimmy to manipulate and lie to Chuck,

then it's wrong for Chuck to manipulate and lie to Jimmy.

Premise 2: It's wrong for Jimmy to manipulate and lie to Chuck.

Therefore,

Conclusion: It's wrong for Chuck to manipulate and lie to Jimmy.

Notice, our two examples here – involving Daniel Ocean and Jimmy/Chuck – are different in a number of ways. The argument concerning Daniel Ocean has twice the number of premises as the argument concerning Jimmy and Chuck. Also, the argument concerning Jimmy and Chuck is about a moral judgment (i.e. whether or not a certain action is morally wrong), while the argument concerning Daniel Ocean is simply about a straightforwardly factual matter about whether or not a particular person (Daniel Ocean) performed a particular action (robbing the Bellagio Hotel and Casino). Nevertheless, what they have in common is that they are each arguments. They both attempt to establish an idea as true (i.e. the conclusion) based on a set of evidence or reasons (i.e. the premises).

For better or worse, we rarely see arguments in the world laid out so plainly as the arguments we have here. Unless you are reading a fairly precise piece of philosophy, hardly anyone lists out their premises as we see in our initial two examples, and almost no one comes right out and says "And therefore, my conclusion is...!" Because of this, perhaps without realizing it, we are confronted with arguments on a daily, if not a minute-by-minute basis. Most (if not all) television commercials contain an argument, the conclusion of which is typically something like "You should absolutely purchase the product and/or service we just happen to be selling!" When a politician is campaigning for votes, or introducing a new piece of legislation, he or she is making an argument. When scientists gather data, formulate and test hypotheses, and on that basis arrive at a conclusion, they are making an argument. When you are prioritizing your day and trying to decide which tasks need to be completed, and which tasks can be put off until later in the week, you are making an argument to *yourself*.

We should care about arguments because we care about the truth. We all want to arrive at and believe what is true. And of course, we all want to avoid believing what is false. Because of this, it's important to think hard about arguments. So, throughout this book, we'll try to develop the skills to better recognize, analyze, and evaluate arguments.

Argument Recognition

When someone is trying to persuade you to believe something by presenting you with an argument, they rarely come out and say so. They rarely say "My conclusion is _____, and my premises are (or, my evidence is) _____." Because of this, before we can evaluate arguments as good or bad (or rational or irrational), we'll have to first develop the skill of recognizing arguments and then *analyzing* them. To give **analysis** of something it to study it by breaking it down into its parts.

We've already given a very brief analysis of arguments when we pointed out that they have two parts: premises and a conclusion. Both premises and conclusions must be propositions. A **proposition** is the idea expressed by a declarative sentence. It is an idea that is either true or false.

Consider the idea of respect or the idea of love. These are not propositions because love is neither true nor false. Respect is neither true nor false. However, consider the claim "Walter respects Gus." or "Hank loves Marie." The ideas (i.e. propositions) expressed by these sentences are the types of things that are either true or false. This is an important fact when it comes to recognizing (and analyzing) arguments. Premises and conclusions must be propositions. They cannot be questions or commands. A premise of an argument cannot be "Will it rain tomorrow?" That said, the premise of an argument *could* be "We don't know whether or not it will rain tomorrow."

because "We don't know whether or not it will rain tomorrow." is the type of thing that is either true or false. Similarly, the conclusion of an argument cannot be "Vote for John Jackson on Election Day!" Again, a command (or request) is neither true nor false. However, the claim "You should vote for John Jackson on Election Day!" or "It is in our collective best interest for you to vote for John Jackson on Election Day." could be the conclusion of an argument because these are the types of things that are either true or false.

It's worth pointing out that when someone asks "Will it rain tomorrow?" it is not uncommon that they intend to express a proposition. They may ask the question for the purposes of pointing out the fact "We don't know whether or not it will rain tomorrow." Likewise, when someone makes the request or command "Vote for John Jackson on Election Day!" They may intend to assert the proposition that "You *should* vote for John Jackson." or "It is in our collective best interest for you to vote for John Jackson." If someone is clearly attempting to craft an argument, and in so doing they ask a question or make a request (or command), it is *possible* that they are attempting to *implicitly* express a proposition. That said, it is still the case that the question or command *themselves* are neither premises nor conclusions of arguments.

So, when we are on the lookout for an argument, we are looking for premises and a conclusion. And, premises and conclusions must be propositions – ideas that are either true or false. While most of us aren't in the habit of labeling our premises and conclusion as such, here's a bit of good news. We do have words that we often use that *indicate* that we are about to express a premise or a conclusion. We can call these premise indicators and conclusion indicators. Perhaps the most common conclusion indicator is the word "therefore". When someone uses "therefore", what is almost certainly to follow is the conclusion of an argument. A popular premise indicator is "since". Below, see the non-exhaustive list of premise indicators and conclusion indicators.

Premise Indicators		
Since	Supposing that	As
Because	Assuming that	In that
Given That	For	In view of the fact that

Conclusion Indicators		
Therefore	Consequently	It must be the case that
Thus	Hence	It follows
Ergo	So	Which means that

Exercise 1.1

Arguments have two parts: premises and a conclusion. Each of the following passages contains an argument. Determine what the premises of the argument are and what the conclusion is. Our lists of premise indicators and conclusion indicators will be helpful here, but not every set of premises is marked with a premise indicator; not every conclusion marked with a conclusion indicator.

Example:

"It is clear that college athletes are treated like employees; without the student-athletes, the NCAA would not exist. Thus, athletes should receive their fair share of the spoils generated by the work they put in."[1]

---

1 Gilbert (2017).

Answer:

Premise: It is clear that college athletes are treated like employees.

Premise: Without the student-athletes, the NCAA would not exist.

Conclusion: Athletes should receive their fair share of the spoils generated by the work they put in.

Example:

Despite what you see in the movies, computers will never be intelligent in the way that human beings are intelligent given that human beings actually know and understand things: we have our own subjective perspective on the world. Our intelligence is more than an ability to take in and spit out information. In contrast, computers are nothing more than devices for storing 1's and 0's that can produce a particular output in response to a particular input.

Answer:

Premise: Human beings actually know and understand things: we have our own subjective perspective on the world.

Premise: Our intelligence is more than an ability to take in and spit out information.

Premise: Computers are nothing more than devices for storing 1's and 0's that can produce a particular output in response to a particular input.

Conclusion: Computers will never be intelligent in the way that human beings are intelligent

1. The so called "War on Drugs" has failed in this country. Given that the War on Drugs has imprisoned (and made felons of) thousands of people for non-violent offenses, made killers (like those in the drug cartels) enormously wealthy and powerful, and still failed to make most drugs inexpensive or hard to get. The outcome of the War on Drugs is readily apparent.

2. "An agreement cannot bind unless both parties to the agreement know what they are doing and freely choose to do it. This implies that the seller who intends to enter a contract with a customer has a duty to disclose exactly what the customer is buying and what the terms of the sale are."[2]

3. "It is certain and obvious to the senses, that in this world some things are moved. But everything that is moved is moved by another... But this does not go on to infinity. For if it did, then there would not be any first mover and as a result, none of the others would effect motion, either... Therefore, one has to arrive at some first mover that is not being moved by anything. And this is what everyone takes to be God."[3]

4. We must pass a constitutional amendment *repealing* the 2nd amendment! The founding fathers only added the right to bear arms because they were afraid of King George (or people like him) taking over the country and establishing a tyrannical rule. We've now maintained a thriving democracy for almost 250 years; King George isn't exactly a threat any more. Because of that, and the problem with gun violence in this country, the conclusion is clear.

5. "I think, therefore I am."[4]

---

2   Velasquez (2005).
3   Aquinas (1276).
4   Descartes (1993).

6. A superhero – by definition – is a person with a super-human power who uses that power for the good of mankind. Granted, Batman is *very* powerful. He's got practically unlimited financial resources. He's maybe the world's greatest detective. And, he seems to be some sort of ninja. That said, none of these powers are super-human, even when taken together! So, Batman is not a superhero.

7. *The Last Jedi* was a terrible movie. In view of the facts that the humor in it was juvenile, the main plot was basically just a slow police car chase in space, and it contains a scene that completely breaks the universe. I don't see how anyone could come to any other conclusion.

8. "Forebear to judge, for we are sinners all."[5]

9. "Poetry is finer and more philosophical than history; for poetry expresses the universal and history only the particular."[6]

10. "The fence around the cemetery is foolish, for those inside can't get out and those outside don't want to get in."[7]

11. "Natural selection is interested in behavior, not in the truth of belief, except as that latter is related to behavior. So, concede for the moment that natural selection might perhaps be expected to produce creatures with cognitive faculties that are reliable when it comes to beliefs about the physical environment... But what about beliefs that go far beyond anything with survival

---

5 Shakespeare (1591).
6 Aristotle (1997).
7 Brisbane (1924).

value? It follows – in a wonderful irony – that a materialistic naturalist should be skeptical about science."[8]

12. A casserole is – by definition – a baked food item that is both baked and served in rectangular-prism-shaped glass or metal dishware. It often contains varying combinations of meat, cheese, and some sort of grain. A lasagna is an *Italian* baked food item that is both baked and served in rectangular-prism-shaped glass or metal dishware. It traditionally contains some combination of meat, cheese, and pasta (i.e. a grain). So, as weird as it is to say, a lasagna is a casserole.

13. Today, Major League Baseball players train year-around and are some of the finest athletes on the planet. Major League pitchers throw (on average) ten to fifteen miles per hour faster than they did 100 years ago, and the contemporary use of bullpens means that hitters face fewer fatigued pitchers in the later innings. As hard as it is to admit, if Babe Ruth were playing today, he wouldn't be anywhere near the star that he was in his day.

14. "Changes are real. Now, changes are only possible in time, and therefore time must be something real."[9]

15. Physicalism is the view that all that exists is the physical world, that there is nothing more to or outside of space and time as we know it. This, some confess, is spooky if not depressing proposition. For, if all that exists is the physical world, then all that you and I are (or any person is) is merely a complex collection of atoms. What would it even mean to say that it is wrong for one complex collection of atoms to do something to (e.g. steal, lie to, or even kill)

---

8   Plantinga (2012).
9   Kant (2010).

another complex collection of atoms? Nothing. Such a sentiment would be vacuous. It would be meaningless. So, if physicalism is true, nothing is right and nothing is wrong (nothing is good, and nothing is bad).

16. "Student athletes could have the best of both worlds. The NCAA could continue to ban salaries being given to student athletes, and instead relax some of the other standards they impose on them. Let these students be sponsored by companies. Let them appear in ads on TV. Let them earn money in all of those other ways that professional athletes support themselves. It wouldn't create a logistical nightmare, it wouldn't affect the integrity of the game. It would give teams some flexibility in how to attract new players, and it would give athletes some incentives to stay in school."[10]

17. T-shirts are wet. Towels are wet. These are the types of things that can be wet. Water is not wet. Wetness is property of things when they are covered by or saturated with water. Water is never covered in or saturated with itself.

18. "Death... the most awful of evils, is nothing to us, seeing that, when we are, death is not come, and, when death is come, we are not."[11]

19. "He that loveth not knoweth not God; for God is love."[12]

20. Some have argued that one's duties and obligations are completely reducible to his or her cultural values. That is, whether or not it is wrong to do something is entirely determined by the norms of one's culture – call this view "Cultural Relativism". However, if this is true, then those who are most regularly

---

10 Editors (2017).
11 Epicurus (1966)
12 1 John 4:8 (KJV).

thought of as paragons of virtue – Gandhi, Martin Luther King Jr., and even Jesus – are actually *villains*, because each one of these men were staunchly pitted *against* the values and norms of their culture. Insofar as it seems counterintuitive to call Gandhi, Martin Luther King Jr., or Jesus a villain, that's a reason for thinking that Cultural Relativism is false.

21. What does "Beauty is in the eye of the beholder." even mean? It could only mean that there is no actual property of beauty out in the world. Beauty is just the way something (e.g. a "beautiful" painting, statue, or song) makes you feel, *subjectively*. But, if that is the case, if beauty really *is* in the eye of the beholder, then the sound I make when I throw a snare drum down a flight of stairs has no more actual aesthetic value than Handel's "Messiah" or "Hey Jude" by the Beatles. This, I must think, is quite absurd. So, beauty is not in the eye of the beholder.

22. St. Louis Cardinals legend Stan Musial has more hits in the history of Major League Baseball than all but 3 people (i.e. Pete Rose, Ty Cobb, and Hank Aaron). He was selected to 20 all star teams. He's 11th all time in Wins-Above-Replacement, and he finished his career with 475 home runs. However, he *also* holds the distinction of being the most underrated player of all time. Because, despite these accomplishments, in 1999, he was not voted onto Major League Baseball's All-Century Team (he had to be added to it after the vote by a panel of experts).

23. Mrs. Peacock was searching the cellar when the Singing Telegram girl was shot, so she could not have been the murderer.

24. "In most states that have implemented teacher evaluations, nearly all teachers perform at or above expectations. Additionally, states already use 'multiple measures' to evaluate teachers. There are literally no states that use

only test scores in their evaluations. The truth is, it's nearly impossible for a teacher to get fired because of poor test scores... Poor test results may be embarrassing when released publicly... But the claims of massive stakes driven by federal or state law[s which implement teacher evaluations based on student testing] are overwrought."[13]

25. "There must be simple substances because there are composites; for a composite is nothing else than a collection or aggregation of simple substances."[14]

26. It is important that offensive, even bigoted speech is protected. The reason is that suppressing such speech does not stop people from holding offensive, bigoted views. When offensive, bigoted views are allowed to be freely expressed, only then can they be met with calm, rational argumentation and shown to be wrongheaded and altogether false.

27. Whenever a Republican President is in office and something good happens (e.g. the economy is doing well), the Republican Party heaps credit onto the President for the accomplishment. Likewise, whenever something bad happens (e.g. the economy is in shambles), the Democrats are quick to assign the President blame for the failure. And, unsurprisingly, the exact (opposite) happens when a Democratic is holding the office. So, it seems clear that, as Matthew Yglesias has put it: "The reality is that no president deserves as much credit or blame as he gets from the mass public for growth trends during his administration."[15]

---

13 Huffman (2015).
14 Leibniz (1991).
15 Yglesias (1990).

28. "To safeguard one's happiness is a duty, at least indirectly; for discontent with one's condition amidst the press of worries and unsatisfied wants may easily become a great *temptation to the transgression of duties.*"[16]

29. If mathematics is merely an invention, then if human beings (or similar enough creatures) had never existed, then "2 + 2 = 4" would not be true. But, I cannot imagine a world in which "2 + 2 = 4" is false; even in worlds where no intelligent creatures exist, it still seems like "2 + 2 = 4" would have to be true. So, mathematics is not merely an invention.

30. The creators of *The Simpsons* must have some sort of psychic power. Over the course of the show's run, they have correctly predicted (among other things) that the Fox Corporation will be taken over by Disney, that MIT professor Bengt Holmström would win a Nobel Prize, that Siegfried and Roy will suffer an attack from one of their show tigers, and (perhaps most surprisingly of all) that Donald Trump would one day be President of the United States.[17]

31. Over the past decades the trend has been clear. More and more jobs have become automated. Recently, even white-color jobs – such as the work of lawyers, accountants, and bankers – have been replaced by nothing more than clever lines of code. There's no reason to think that this will trend will slow down any time soon. If it doesn't, there will be a small percentage of people who own the computers and robots that are doing all the work, and a large percentage of the population with nothing to do all day (to earn a living anyway). Because of this, the government needs to be thinking seriously about a universal basic income for all of its citizens.

---

16 Kant (1954).
17 Wittmer (2018).

32. "Venus and Mercury must revolve around the sun, because of their never moving far away from it, and because of their being seen now beyond it and now on the side of it."[18]

33. Many studies show that students who take courses from professors they rate poorly on teacher-evaluations actually do *better* in subsequent classes. And of course, we shouldn't find this surprising. Students are more likely to give high marks to professors who go easy on them. Ergo, poor teacher-evaluations do not equate to good evidence that a professor is actually doing poorly in the classroom.

34. "An author's creation is his property, and copyright simply vindicates the author's natural rights and prevents the unauthorized exploitation of the author's work. The rights which copyright afford the author are, thus, not a privilege or some type of reward."[19]

35. When someone makes a lucky guess, we wouldn't say that they *knew* the right answer, that they had *knowledge*. If you are stumped by a math problem and hastily right down an answer "42". If the correct answer *turns out to be* 42, we wouldn't credit you with having *known* that the answer is 42. Similarly, if a person believes something simply based on wishful thinking, say, that their wedding day (months from now) will not be on a rainy day. Even if it doesn't rain on said wedding day, we wouldn't say that the bride or groom *knew* that it wouldn't rain on their wedding day. Ergo, while arriving at the truth might be necessary for knowledge, it is not sufficient.

36. Some have argued that a hot dog is not a sandwich on the basis that 1) "to sandwich" means to enclose one object between two additional objects and yet

---

18 Galilei (2001).
19 Karjiker (2013).

2) a traditionally served hot dog is not enclosed between two things (e.g. two pieces of bread). It is rather served by placing it *into* one particular thing (a single hot dog bun). Yet, many sandwiches (such as hoagies) are served *within* a single bun-like bread product. The meat, vegetables, etc. are not placed between two pieces of bread, but (instead) within a single piece of bread product. So, if a hot dog is not a sandwich (on the grounds mentioned here), then a hoagie is not a sandwich.

37. To say something false is not necessarily to be lying. For if it were, then every time you answer a question incorrectly in your logic course, that would mean you are lying.[20]

38. It is completely reasonable for the state to make certain baby names illegal. The government has a well established history – with widespread social support – of intervening when parents abuse or neglect their children. Parents who name their child some nonsense string of characters, after their favorite band like "Metallica", or after a moral monster like Adolf Hitler[21] are clearly not considering the long term well-being of their child to the point of neglect.

39. When a person claims that they were the victim of a crime, skeptics too often respond by suggesting that they cannot move forward with a trial or even an investigation because there is "no evidence". However, this is misleading at best and plainly false at worst. It is not the case that there is literally *no* (i.e. as in zero) evidence because the testimony of the alleged victim is itself evidence.

40. "Athletes are going to take steroids and turn to doping regardless of the

---

20 Of course, it may be the case that you never **do** answer a question incorrectly in your logic course. If this turns out to be the case: hey. Nice job.

21 These examples come from real world cases in which actual parents attempted to name their child in a (let's call it) unique manner. See Debczak (2017) and Osborne (2018).

rules. Drug use in cycling is seemingly as old as the sport itself, and baseball players have tried to cut corners wherever possible, whether it be with spit balls, corked bats, stimulants or steroids. It doesn't justify the actions of [athletes who have taken banned substances], but the current system has continually failed to establish a level playing field for the world's most talented athletes. Legalizing steroids, doping and other performance enhancers would finally set an even bar, and that would just be the first of many benefits."[22]

Enthymemes

In the previous section, we pointed out that when making an argument, it isn't terribly common for people to lay out their premises and conclusion in a clear and precise manner. It is much more common for people to deliver their arguments in a perhaps less precise but more easily digestible ways like a speech or in an essay in the op-ed section of a newspaper. Because of this, recognizing an analyzing arguments can sometimes present us with challenges. With that in mind, here's one additional challenge. Sometimes, we don't even explicitly express every one of our assumptions (i.e. premises). When we do this, we are crafting an argument known as an enthymeme. An **enthymeme** is an argument with at least one premise that is not explicitly stated. That is, it is an argument in which at least one premise is left *unstated*.

The reason that we craft arguments this way is fairly straightforward. Often, it is fairly clear what assumptions we are taking for granted when we succinctly compose or express an argument. Consider the following enthymeme.

Harrison Ford has never won an Academy Award, so he cannot be considered a truly great actor.

---

22 Smith (2012).

Forget for the time being whether or not this is a good argument (it probably isn't). The point here is that it has a missing or unstated premise. The person making this argument obviously intends to imply an additional assumption: that *only actors who have won an Academy Award should be considered truly great*. Of course, sometimes, we don't come out and express every single one of our assumptions (i.e. premises) because they aren't all that intuitive, and saying them out loud will only highlight this fact. However, we often leave certain assumptions unstated because it is simply unnecessary to explicitly state them; almost anyone who is to hear the argument will understand that there is an additional, implied assumption. Here's one more example.

Since I am against any and all forms of cruel and unusual punishment, I cannot justify any government's use of sleep-deprivation on its prisoners.

The implied premise here is of course that sleep-deprivation is a form of cruel and unusual punishment. In almost every context, one making this argument should feel confident that those within earshot would naturally understand this unstated premise to be a part of the argument.

Sometimes enthymemes are fairly straightforward. That is, sometimes when people express arguments they needn't list each and every one of the premises of their argument explicitly because those premises will be naturally understood to be a part of the argument. However, this is not always the case. Sometimes, there are enthymemes for which it is not immediately obvious what the implicit premise(s) is (are). For this reason, it will be worth our time to practice recognizing (and making explicit) the implicit assumptions of some enthymemes.

Exercise 1.2

The following passages are all enthymemes: they are arguments with at least one implicit, or unstated premise. For each example, identify the (or, an important) unstated premise.

Example:

Betty is a fairly self-absorbed person, so it's unlikely that she'll volunteer to help organize the canned-food drive.

Answer:

Unstated Premise: Self-absorbed people volunteer less on average.

Example:

Chicago should not be the host city for the next Summer Olympics since they are unwilling to build new venues for each event (they want to reuse old / existing venues).

Answer:

Unstated Premise: The host city for the next Summer Olympics should be willing to build new venues for each event.

1. Whoever strangled Yvette (the maid) must have been fairly strong. So, Mrs. Peacock couldn't have done it.

2. Dan Marino, Barry Bonds, and Charles Barkley never won a championship in

their respective sports, so none of them can be considered a truly great athlete.

3. Professor Coppenger gets especially complimentary evaluations from his students every semester. He must be a really great instructor.

4. Tigers are mammals, because they are cats.

5. Tom Hanks lives in California, because he lives in Los Angeles.

6. "He would not take the crown. Therefore, 'tis certain he was not ambitious."[23]

7. Everything in the house is completely functional. Nothing is broken – it all works exactly as it is designed to work. The worst thing someone could say is that the 1960's decorum and styling is outdated. So, no improvements or updates need to be made to the house.

8. Santa Claus only brings presents to nice little boys and girls, so Damien won't be getting anything this Christmas.

9. Barry Bonds should never be elected into the Baseball Hall of Fame since he was a rabid steroid user.

10. Yadier Molina should be elected into the Baseball Hall of Fame since he has won multiple Gold Glove Awards.

11. All men are mortal. Therefore, Socrates is mortal.

12. Philosophy is not a subject matter in one of the S.T.E.M. fields, so it's probably not a good idea to major in philosophy.

---

23 Shakespeare (1623).

13. Dr. Jones won't grade our papers *that* hard. Right? After all, he's such a nice guy.

14. *Said in a condescending tone*: "Of course your new car broke down after just a week; it's a Ford!"

15. I refuse to defend an unjust war, and for that reason, I cannot and will not defend the Vietnam War.

16. A troll is a person on the internet who says things (usually anonymously) simply to provoke a reaction out of people (usually a reaction of anger or frustration). So, George Will isn't a troll.

17. Like the song says, "We don't smoke marijuana in Muskogee." Ergo, Conway Twitty does not smoke marijuana.

18. If the death penalty doesn't deter violent crime, there is no justifiable reason for having the death penalty. Therefore, the death penalty is immoral and should be abolished immediately.

19. Because the game of chess does not require of its participants to fully engage their body in any athletic manner, chess is not a sport.

20. Tony Stark / Ironman doesn't have any superpowers. Like Bruce Wayne / Batman, he's just a rich guy who can buy impressive (or build) military-grade crime fighting weapons. Therefore, Tony Stark / Ironman is not a superhero.

21. Josef is a philosophy major, so he's likely very opinionated.

22. Since John isn't much of a science-fiction fan (he's more into fantasy), he

probably won't like Star Wars.

23. This much should be obvious: pineapple (of course) is a *fruit*. Hence, pineapple does *not* belong on pizza.

24. I want what is best for the lower and middles classes in this country (those rich fat-cats can fend for themselves). That's why I oppose capitalism!

25. I want to see each and every child in this school district achieve their maximal potential. That's why we need more standardized testing!

26. Dr. Heter owns a lot of books, so he must be very well-read.

27. We must ensure that U.S. Presidential elections are just and fair. Therefore, we must abandon the electoral college.

28. The Rams don't have an elite defense, so they won't be winning the Super Bowl this year.

29. You can't win a Presidential Election without winning either Ohio or Florida, so President Whitmore won't be winning reelection in November.

30. Ted is almost certainly against the legalization of Marijuana, given that he's a Republican.

Arguments and Explanations

Part of developing the skill of recognizing and analyzing arguments is developing the skill of knowing when we *aren't* being presented an argument. Remember, an argument is a set of premises and a conclusion. Premises are supposed to be evidence for or reasons to believe a conclusion.

Put differently, arguments are attempts to *establish* that their conclusions are true. That said, some things that look like arguments are not in fact arguments. What can sometimes be mistaken for an argument is an explanation. Here's one way to think of the distinction between arguments and explanations.

> <u>Argument</u>: arguments attempt to make the case *that* some idea is true.
> <u>Explanation</u>: explanations attempt to give an account of *why* some idea is true.

When a claim is in dispute, when it is a matter of disagreement, an argument is appropriate. And, if people are approaching the dispute appropriately, they will attempt to establish that their position is true by presenting a good argument for it. In contrast, when an idea is *not* in dispute or when an idea can be taken for granted, an argument is not necessary. However, in such a case, we still might search out an explanation for why the idea is true.

Part of the reason it can be all too easy to mistake explanations for arguments is that explanations can use some of the same language that we commonly associate with arguments such as premise indicators like "since" and "because" and conclusion indicators such as "therefore" and "so". Also, explanations can have a structure similar to arguments. Where as arguments have premises and a conclusion, explanations have what are sometimes called the "explanandum" (i.e. the explanation itself) and the "explanans" (the idea or phenomenon that is being explained).

Consider the following examples.

"[Pete Rose] belongs in Major League Baseball's Hall of Fame. He belongs there not only because he was one of the great players of his day. Not only because he broke Ty Cobb's record for most hits in a

career. Not only because he played with the kind of abandon and enthusiasm of a child. Pete Rose belongs in the Hall of Fame because Rose's sin – betting on baseball – is nothing compared with the sins of the steroid era or baseball's long, lax and disgusting attitude toward the far more heinous problem of domestic violence."[24]
- E.J. Montini "I hate Pete Rose (who Belongs in the Hall of Fame)"

"The 77-year-old [Pete] Rose has been *persona non grata* in Major League Baseball since 1989 when he was banned for allegedly betting on games during his tenure as manager of the Cincinnati Reds. He subsequently applied for reinstatement [unsuccessfully] on three occasions... One of the biggest impediments for reinstatement has been Rose himself, as the 17-time All-Star has never admitted to betting against his own team and has continued actively betting on baseball in retirement. His lack of contrition has been problematic for the succession of MLB Commissioners who has come into power during his exile."[25]
- Ryan Murphy, "Odds Against Pete Rose Being Eligible for Baseball Hall of Fame by 2020"

The first passage is an argument. The author is clearly attempting to establish the truth of a conclusion – that Pete Rose should be in the Baseball Hall of Fame – by providing evidence as he points out that Pete Rose had one of the greatest baseball careers of all time and that many people in baseball have done things much worse than what Pete Rose did (i.e. betting on baseball).

The second passage, however, is not an argument. It is an explanation. The author is merely trying to give an account for why it is that Pete Rose has not been reinstated in baseball. This is a well established fact (that Pete Rose

---

24 Montini (2015).
25 Murphy (2018).

was banned from baseball and has not been granted reinstatement). It is not a matter of dispute, so it is not the type of thing that would need to be argued for.

It's worth pointing out that it might not be immediately obvious whether some passages should be thought of as an argument or an explanation. In fact, some passages can be thought of as containing both an argument as well as an explanation. Consider the following example.

> "'Baby, It's Cold Outside' is a song ahead of its time — released a full twenty years before the sexual revolution for women — and it celebrates a feminist taking control of her own sexual choices. The only reason to ban the song is to pit progressives against conservatives. Speaking for one liberal feminist, I will continue to appreciate the song for the anthem that it is."[26]
> - Marney White, "Drinking, Smoking, Carousing: Why 'Baby it's Cold Outside' is actually a Feminist Anthem"

On an initial reading, we might think that the passage is straightforwardly an explanation. The author is simply attempting to account for why it is *she* will continue to appreciate the song "Baby it's Cold Outside". We can just take her word for it that this is true, that she will continue to appreciate the song. This is of course not the type of thing she would need to establish with an argument.

On the other hand, it is unlikely that this is all that the author wishes to communicate here. She is – in all likelihood – attempting to argue in a round about way that the song really *is* something that *should* be appreciated (perhaps by everyone). So, this passage can be thought of as containing both an argument as well as an explanation. Explicitly, the author is explaining *her* support; implicitly, she is attempting to make a case that her reader should be supportive as well.

---

26 White (2018).

30

The lesson here is that whether or not a passage should be thought of as an argument or explanation is dependent upon its purpose. Is the author attempting to establish a conclusion based on evidence (i.e. by giving an argument)? Or, is the author attempting to give an account of an already established fact (i.e. by giving an explanation)? The answers to these questions in any given example is the key to determining whether or not what is being presented is an argument or an explanation.

Exercise 1.3

Each of the following passages contains either an argument or an explanation. For each example, determine whether the passage is an argument or an explanation. If the passage is an argument, determine what the conclusion of the argument is. If the passage is an explanation, determine what the fact or idea is that is being explained. Then, offer a brief justification why the passage should be thought of as either an argument or an explanation. If a passage could reasonably be thought of as containing both an argument as well as an explanation, indicate this and be able to justify your answer.

> Example: "Interestingly, pizza was recently ranked as the food most associated with indicators of addiction according to a recent study. But what is it specifically about pizza that makes it so universally craved?... The psychological response to pizza's ingredient combinations is partially explained by the fact that highly processed foods like pizza, with added amounts of fat, refined carbohydrates and salt, are most associated with behavioral indicators of addiction, such as loss of control over consumption, cravings, and continued consumption despite negative consequences."[27]
>
> - Lisa Drayer, "Why is Pizza so Addictive?"

---

27 Drayer (2018).

Answer:

Argument or explanation: Explanation

Idea being explained: We eat a lot of pizza. / Pizza is popular.

Justification: The main idea behind in the passage is that pizza is a highly consumed food product. This is widely known and not something that hardly anyone would need to be persuaded to believe. Thus, the author is merely attempting to explain why it is that pizza is so popular.

Example:

"While community colleges should always be committed to continuous improvement, they often get a bum rap on quality. For one thing, measures such as degree-completion rates are notoriously uninformative. Although transfer students can — and ought to — receive associate degrees from their colleges before heading off to universities, large numbers of them do not even fill out the necessary paperwork."[28]
- John Hood "Community Colleges Deserve Better"

Answer:

Argument or explanation: Argument

Conclusion: Community Colleges often get a bum rap.

Justification: The author is attempting to establish that the reputation

---

28 Hood (2018).

community colleges get is often undeserved. This is something that is (likely) a matter of debate and not easily demonstrable. So, in order to establish this conclusion, he presents the evidence that degree completion and transfer data is poorly collected (thus, low degree completion and transfer *data* are not in fact good evidence of *actual* low degree completion or transfers).

1. "Studies of student behavior and attributes show a majority of students violate standards of academic integrity to some degree, and that high achievers are just as likely to do it as others. Moreover, there is evidence that the problem has worsened over the last few decades. Experts say the reasons are relatively simple: Cheating has become easier and more widely tolerated, and both schools and parents have failed to give students strong, repetitive messages about what is allowed and what is prohibited."[29]

- Richard Perez-Pena, "Studies Find More Students Cheating"

2. "Rather than trying to protect students from words and ideas that they will inevitably encounter, colleges should do all they can to equip students to thrive in a world full of words and ideas that they cannot control. One of the great truths taught by Buddhism (and Stoicism, Hinduism, and many other traditions) is that you can never achieve happiness by making the world conform to your desires. But you can master your desires and habits of thought."[30]

- Greg Lukianoff and Jonathan Haidt, "The Coddling of the American Mind".

3. "The testing environment has placed school-aged youngsters under unnecessary stress, provoking fear and inducing bouts of panic, crying spells, apathy, sleeplessness and depression. It is for this and other reasons that —

---

29 Perez-Pena (2012).
30 Lukianoff and Haidt (2015).

along with other esteemed educational organizations – the American Educational Research Association, the National Association for the Education of Young Children and the Association of Childhood Education International – have denounced the overuse of standardized testing."[31]

> \- James D. Kirylo, "What if we Skipped over Testing Season?"

4. "Two years after it became clear that fake news improperly influenced the 2016 U.S. presidential election, Facebook and other social networks are still being excoriated for not effectively combating the problem. While it's true that Facebook has mismanaged its response, continuing to berate the company ignores a fundamental truth: Fake news has become too pervasive for any one organization to obliterate on its own. It's time for the public to help."[32]

> \- Kara Alaimo, "Want to Purge Fake News? Try Crowdsourcing"

5. "At the end of the day, the ones who shoulder the real responsibility are the [NFL] players. Therefore, the drive for safer [football] equipment should begin with them. It is their health that is at risk, and they are the ones making a conscious decision to be exposed to potential injuries each time they step onto the field. No one is putting a gun to their heads and making them play football. They *choose* to play."[33]

> \- Nathan Risinger, "The Ethics of Football Helmets"

6. "Another reason we may think our dogs are gifted stems from the way we view ourselves. When people are asked to rate themselves on traits such as intelligence, they tend to give above-average ratings. This *Lake Wobegon effect* —named after the fictional town created by Garrison Keillor where "all the children are above average" — extends to pets. In a study published in *Basic*

---

31 Kirylo (2017).
32 Alaimo (2018).
33 Risinger (2012).

and Applied Social Psychology, researchers had 137 pet owners rate both their own pet and the average pet on a range of traits, including intelligence. The results revealed that the people rated their pets as above average on desirable traits and below average on undesirable traits."[34]

> - David Z. Hambrick, "Your Dog May not be a Genius, After All"

7. "Many studies show that students who take courses from professors they rate poorly on teacher-evaluations actually do *better* in subsequent classes. And of course, we shouldn't find this surprising. Students are more likely to give high marks to professors who go easy on them."[35]

> - Joshua S. Heter, *Logic: A Guided Introduction*

8. "Schools that changed their policy from allowing cell phones to prohibiting them saw student test scores improve by 6.41%, according to a 2015 study of the United Kingdom. In the US, administrators of schools that have adopted 'away for the day' policies have reported improvements in students' emotional well-being too... It is time we follow France's lead and do what is best for our middle school students today. That means require all middle school students to put their phones 'away for the day'."[36]

> - Delaney Ruston, "Smartphones aren't a Smart Choice in Middle School"

9. "With few exceptions (e.g. extreme want or necessity), it is considered morally blameworthy to steal another's property. In the most obvious cases, I have harmed you in some way by taking what is yours. For example, if you own a pear and I come along and steal your pear, then I have deprived you of some good that was rightfully yours. You can no longer enjoy it. If you worked for it,

---

34 Hambrick (2018).

35 Heter (2021).

36 Ruston (2017).

then your work was for naught. And this highlights one of the key features of property rights – physical excludability."[37]

> - Andrew T. Forcehimes, "Download this Essay: A Defence of Stealing Ebooks"

10. "There is enough money to fund public colleges, simply through redistribution of funds. A few public policy changes could provide the necessary funds to pay for this program. Raising the capital gains tax, as well as the tax put on Wall Street slightly higher would cover the cost easily. Though some may view the idea as fiscally irresponsible, it is an investment in the American people. Having more people with a college education would serve to benefit the country as a whole. It's time students have access to the education they deserve, and for the United States to catch up with the rest of the Western world."[38]

> - Carlos Alejandro De Los Santos, "The Need for Tuition Free College."

11. "The debate about hate speech has been long and contentious in part because it requires us to examine two of our deepest values – equality and free speech – in a setting in which they are in tension with one another."[39]

> - Richard Delgado and Jean Stefancic, "Four Observations about Hate Speech"

12. "Montana voted to [to do what South Dakota just did: restore a traditional, conservative interest rate limit of 36 percent per annum] a few years earlier. In both [Montana and South Dakota], re-establishing the traditional usury limits that were the norm through most of American history is working just fine. The

---

37 Forcehimes (2013).
38 De Los Santos (2018).
39 Delgado and Stefancic (2009).

public still has access to credit cards, personal loans, home mortgages and even pawnshop credit. And banks and credit unions were hardly affected at all. The Utah Legislature should not wait for Washington to protect struggling families from usurious credit. And if the Utah Legislature will not act, then maybe the public should."[40]

> - Josh Kanter and Christopher L. Peterson, "Utah Families need Payday Lending Reform"

13. "Today's dominant approach to [Artificial Intelligence] has not worked out. Yes, some remarkable applications have been built from it, including Google Translate and Google Duplex. But the limitations of these applications as a form of intelligence should be a wake-up call. If machine learning and big data can't get us any further than a restaurant reservation, even in the hands of the world's most capable [Artificial Intelligence] company, it is time to reconsider that strategy."[41]

> - Gary Marcus, "A.I. is Harder than you Think"

14. "When the government 'taxes' citizens, what this means is that the government demands money from each citizen, under a threat of force: if you do not pay, armed agents hired by the government will take you away and lock you in a cage. This looks like about as a clear a case as any of taking people's property without consent. So the government is a thief. This conclusion is not changed by the fact that the government uses the money for a good cause (if it does so)."[42]

> - Michael Huemer, "Is Taxation Theft?"

---

40 Kanter and Peterson (2017).
41 Marcus (2018).
42 Huemer (2017).

15. "Drunken driving deaths have decreased over the last three decades in large part because we now throw the book at drunken drivers in this country: All 50 states currently define a driver's having a blood-alcohol concentration of 0.08 or higher as a crime; 42 states suspend drivers' licenses on the first offense. Every state also now has some type of ignition interlock law, requiring devices to be installed in the vehicles of convicted drunken drivers that prevent a vehicle from starting if the driver breathes into the device and produces a breath-alcohol level above a preset limit."[43]

    - Mary Kate Cary "Time to Lower the Drinking Age"

16. "Across industries, 45% of organizations claim to experience a problematic shortage of cybersecurity skills. As a result, cybersecurity teams must race from one crisis or breach to the next, with little time for strategic planning or continued learning to keep up with threat sophistication. These are certainly business challenges — and increasingly costly ones at that. The demand itself is driving an expensive bidding war for talent, and the cost of cybercrime is estimated to reach $2.1 trillion by next year... Automation and AI are not eliminating jobs, they are creating them — high-paying, high-level and secure ones at that — at an unprecedented rate."[44]

    - Michael Xie, "AI Doesn't Eliminate Jobs, it Creates them"

17. "There must be simple substances because there are composites; for a composite is nothing else than a collection or aggregation of simple substances."[45]

    - Gottfried Leibniz, *The Monadology*

18. "It's no secret that a college education in America is more expensive than

---

43 Cary (2014).
44 Xie (2018).
45 Leibniz, Ibid.

it's ever been. With tuition at many Universities now exceeding $40,000 *per year*, even a plethora of financial aid opportunities and scholarships leave the average student approaching or upwards of six figures in debt as a result of their four year degree... It's no secret where all the money has gone, though. It's gone to administrative overhead, as that's where the majority of "growth" in colleges have been."[46]

> - Ethan Siegel, "Why College is so Expensive, and How
> to Fix it"

19. "Adopting a national popular vote [as opposed to relying on the electoral college] would trade one set of problems for another... If the national popular vote were the ultimate decider [of the U.S. Presidency], candidates would gravitate toward the voter-rich big cities and their suburbs and ignore everyone else... A popular vote contest involving multiple candidates could produce a winner with say, only 35% of the vote, provoking outcry to create a runoff process involving the top two vote-getters. And if the U.S. popular vote were so close that a nationwide recount were needed, the process could turn into a nightmare dwarfing the Florida fiasco of 2000."[47]

> - The Editorial Board, USA Today, "Keep the Electoral College:
> Our View"

20. "I have struggled, throughout my life, with belief, but the times when I've seen the best evidence for something divine haven't involved sunsets or other miraculous natural displays. No, they've been moments where humans are kind to other humans, even when they don't need to be, when people go out of their way to help, even when there's no reason. Is that because I watched a lot

---

46 Siegel (2016)
47 Editorial Board (2016).

of *Mister Rogers' Neighborhood* growing up? I don't know — but I like to think it might be."[48]

> - Todd VanDerWeff, "9 Times Mister Rogers said Exactly the Right thing"

21. "Social media mobs are not, of course, as pervasive and terrifying as the Communist Party spies. But the Soviet Union is no more, and the mobs are very much with us, so it's their power we need to think about."[49]

> - Megan McArdle, "Living in Fear of the Internet Mob"

22. "In today's era of smartphones and social media, it takes just a few seconds to upload an accusatory photo or video for the world to see, but the ramifications for individuals can last a lifetime... People have long been called out and criticised publicly for breaching social norms... 'If someone jumps the queue in the supermarket, say, they can expect to incur the displeasure of those waiting in line. Arguably, some of this is necessary. What's new today is that technology allows this to be immediately recorded and shared with millions of other unknown internet users thanks to smartphones and social media'."[50]

> - Mark Molloy, "The Dangerous Rise of the Internet Pitchfork Mob"

23. "Barry Bonds and Roger Clemens — I'll lump them together here since the voting electorate [for the Baseball Hall of Fame] does as well. The two are, respectively, the best player and pitcher of their generation. Considering they have received around the same 34-37 percent of votes in their three years on the ballot, most voters still will not look past their known or alleged links to performance-enhancing drugs. I've declined the sheriff's badge and judge's

---

48 VanDerWeff (2018).
49 McArdle (2017).
50 Molloy (2018).

robe when it comes to the morality of Hall of Fame nominees. There are worse scallywags than Bonds and Clemens already in the Hall. I'll keep voting for Clemens and Bonds."[51]

> - Michael Silverman, "Roger Clemons, Barry Bonds get my Vote"

24. "When it comes to the death penalty, there is no acceptable margin of error because a mistake means that an innocent person may be executed. Since 1996, over 150 men have been released from death rows around the country after being exonerated by the results of DNA tests or other evidence. How many innocent people were executed that we did not discover before these advances in forensic science? After years of confronting these decisions myself, I believe there is no longer an adequate justification for an irreversible punishment that does little to make our communities safer."[52]

> - Tim Cole, "It's Wrong for an Imperfect System to Impose an Irreversible Punishment"

25. "Many of the celebratory rituals [of Christmas], as well as the timing of the holiday, have their origins outside of and may predate the Christian commemoration of the birth of Jesus. Those traditions, at their best, have much to do with celebrating human relationships and the enjoyment of the goods that this life has to offer. As an atheist I have no hesitation in embracing the holiday and joining with believers and nonbelievers alike to celebrate what we have in common."[53]

> - John Teehan, "A Holiday Season for Atheists, Too"

26. "If a jury is sufficiently unhappy with the government's case or the government's conduct, it can simply refuse to convict. This possibility puts

---

51 Silverman (2015).
52 Cole (2018).
53 Teehan (2006).

powerful pressure on the state to behave properly. For this reason a jury is one of the most important protections of a democracy."[54]

> - Robert Precht, "Japan the Jury"

27. "Crime has been skyrocketing in China... China's one-child policy is [a potential cause]. While crime has been soaring, the one-child policy, along with a strong preference of Chinese parents for sons over daughters, has resulted in there being approximately 120 boys for every 100 girls... These surplus men, mostly of lower socio-economic status are pouring out of the countryside and into China's industrial cities in search of jobs. Many of them are destined to face tremendous difficulties in finding a wife. Add to this the fact that young unmarried men are the main perpetrators of crime worldwide and commit more than two thirds of violent and property-related crimes in China – and the seeds of a crime explosion are sown."[55]

> - Lisa Cameron, Zhang Dan-dan, and Xin Meng, "China's One- child Policy: Effects on the Sex Ratio and Crime"

28. "What stops many people from photocopying a book and giving it to a pal is not integrity but logistics; it's easier and inexpensive to buy your friend a paperback copy."[56]

> - Randy Cohen, "The Ethicist; I Want my MP3"

29. "What's needed is more time in the classrooms, not less. Our school calendar, with its six-and-a-half hour day and 180-day year, was designed for yesterday's farm economy, not today's high-tech one. While many middle-class families now invest in tutoring and extra learning time, less privileged children

---

54 Precht (2018).
55 Cameron, Dan-dan, and Meng (2018).
56 Cohen (2000).

are left on the sidelines, which only widens the gaps in achievement and opportunity."[57]

    - Luisa A. Ubinas and Chris Gabrieli, "Shortchanged by the Bell"

30. "Humans have been scaring themselves and each other since the birth of the species, through all kinds of methods like storytelling, jumping off cliffs, and popping out to startle each other from the recesses of some dark cave... And we've done this for lots of different reasons – to build group unity, to prepare kids for life in the scary world, and of course, to control behavior. But it's only really in the last few centuries that scaring ourselves for fun (and profit) has become a highly sought-after experience."[58]

    - Margee Kerr, in "The Science of Fear: Why do I like Being Scared?"

Two Types of Arguments

As we've learned so far, arguments have two parts: premises and a conclusion. Arguments have two parts *and* there are two *types* of arguments: deductive arguments and non-deductive arguments. **Deductive arguments** are arguments in which, if the premises are true, the conclusion must be true as well. For deductive arguments, it is impossible for the premises to be true and the conclusion false. Consider the following argument.

    Premise 1: All comedians tell jokes.
    Premise 2: Jerry Seinfeld is a comedian.
    Therefore,
    Conclusion: Jerry Seinfeld tells jokes.

---

57 Ubinas and Gabireli (2011).
58 Feltman (2016).

This is a deductive argument because if the premises are true, the conclusion must be true as well. If it is true that all comedians tell jokes, and if it is also true that Jerry Seinfeld is a comedian, then it must be true that Jerry Seinfeld tells jokes. Suppose Premise 1 is false and not all comedians tell jokes. Perhaps, there is a comedian who doesn't tell jokes; he makes his audience laugh in some other way. This would still be a deductive argument because it would still be true that *if* the premises were true, the conclusion would have to be true as well.

By contrast, **non-deductive arguments** are arguments in which, if the premises are true, the conclusion is merely *more likely* to be true. So, for non-deductive arguments, it is possible for the premises to be true and the conclusion false. Consider the following argument.

Premise 1: Jerry rarely enjoys having dinner with anyone other than George, Elaine, or Kramer.
Premise 2: Kenny often gets on Jerry's nerves.
Therefore,
Conclusion: Jerry will not enjoy having dinner with Kenny.

Again, this is a non-deductive argument because the truth of the premises only makes the conclusion *more likely* to be true. If it is true that Jerry rarely enjoys having dinner with anyone other than George, Elaine, or Kramer, and if it is also true that Kenny often gets on Jerry's nerves, then it is more likely (though of course *not* guaranteed) that Jerry will not enjoy having dinner with Kenny. That is, as this is a non-deductive argument, it *would* be possible for the premises to be true and the conclusion false. At dinner, Jerry could unexpectedly find himself in a good mood, or Kenny could be uniquely charming during dinner with Jerry.

Exercise 1.4

The following passages are arguments. Some of the arguments are deductive arguments; they are arguments such that, if the premises are true, the conclusion must be true. Others are non-deductive arguments. They are arguments such that if the premises are true, that only makes the conclusion more likely to be true. Identify which arguments are deductive and which arguments are non-deductive.

Example:

The St. Louis Blues won the Stanley Cup last year. They brought back essentially the same roster this year. So, the St. Louis Blues will win the Stanley Cup again this year.

Answer:

Deductive or Non-deductive Argument: non-deductive.

This is a non-deductive argument. Even if the premises are true, that does not guarantee that the conclusion is true. If the Blues won the Stanley Cup last year, and they are bringing back the same roster this year. That *might* be good *evidence* that they will repeat as champions, but it certainly does not guarantee that they will the Stanley Cup again.

Example:

The St. Louis Blues are a hockey team with a full roster. All hockey teams with a full roster have at least one goalie. Therefore, the St. Louis Blues have at least one goalie.

Answer:

Deductive or Non-deductive Argument: deductive.

This is a deductive argument. If it is true that all hockey teams with a full roster have at least one goalie, and if it is also true that the St. Louis Blues are a hockey team with a full roster, then it *must* be true that the St. Louis Blues have at least one goalie.

1. We studied workers from 8 different nuclear plants. When it came to plants in Russia, China, the Ukraine, Germany, South Africa, and Argentina, all plant workers at one time or another came down with the disease *Fictionitus*. In two American plants, only about half of the workers caught *Fictionitus*. However, it should be noted that America has the highest safety standards in the world when it comes to exposure for its nuclear plant workers. Therefore, it is a *near* certainty. Unchecked exposure to nuclear energy causes Fictionitus.

2.   Premise 1: All Chicago residents are residents of Illinois.
       Premise 2: Josh is not a resident of Illinois.
       Conclusion: Therefore, Josh is not a Chicago resident.

3.If the universe began to exist, then the universe must have a cause. The universe did in fact begin to exist. If these two assumptions are correct, then it is a certainty. The universe had a cause.

4.   Premise 1: My dog growing up barked.
       Premise 2: Lassie barks (especially when Timmy is in trouble).
       Premise 3: My neighbor's dog barks at me every morning.
       Conclusion: Therefore, all dogs probably bark.

5. Look, all the facts of the case point to Daniel Ocean as being the thief. Mr. Ocean had no recorded income the last three years (even though he's always staying in fancy hotels and wearing expensive suits). He hangs around with a number of shady characters (who, by the way, he met in prison). And, he and his buddies left town, the very day after the heist. So, it is almost a complete certainty that Mr. Ocean is the thief.

6.   Premise 1: My friend Jeff is a Canadian and he loves hockey.
        Premise 2: My neighbor Sam is Canadian and he watches hockey all
        the time.
        Premise 3: This guy I went to school with was from Canada and he
        owned over a dozen hockey jerseys.
        Conclusion: Therefore, chances are, all Canadians like hockey.

7.   Premise 1: Lassie is a mammal.
        Premise 2: All mammals have lungs.
        Conclusion: Therefore, Lassie has lungs.

8. This one thing we know for sure – all men are mortal. And (in case you didn't know), Socrates is a man. If this is all correct, then we know for sure, Socrates is mortal.

9. Don is in the room. Therefore, someone is in the room.

10. Adnan had no known motive to commit the murder, no history of violence, and hardly any window of opportunity to do it. And, his one and only accuser, Jay is a shady character with a propensity for lying. So, Adnan is innocent.

Validity and Soundness

Our focus in this book will largely (though not entirely) be deduction or deductive arguments. There are two primary ways to evaluate deductive arguments: validity and soundness. An argument is **valid** if and only if it follows a proper, deductive form. In other words, an argument is valid if it *really is* a deductive argument. An argument is **sound** if it is valid *and* all of its premises are true. Consider the following argument.

> Premise 1: All readers of Superman Comics have superpowers.
> Premise 2: Jerry is a reader of Superman Comics.
> *Therefore*,
> Conclusion: Jerry has superpowers.

Is this a valid argument? It certainly seems to be a flawed argument, even silly, perhaps. You are likely unaware of any comic book readers who have actual superpowers themselves. However, this argument *is* valid because it follows a proper deductive form. If it *were* true that all readers of Superman comics have superpowers, and if it *were* true that Jerry is a reader of Superman Comics, then it would have to be true that Jerry has superpowers. The flaw in the argument is that it is unsound. That is, even though the argument is valid, it is not sound. Not all of the premises are true; Premise 1 is false. It is not true (perhaps sadly) that all readers of Superman Comics have superpowers themselves. As far as I know, none of them do.

It's important for us to keep the distinction between validity and soundness in mind. Even if someone's assumptions are true, that doesn't mean that what they attempt to infer from those assumptions is also true. Likewise, simply because someone makes a valid argument (i.e. an argument in which if their premises are true, their conclusion follows), that does not mean that they are reasoning from good or true assumptions. We'll proceed here by spending

48

some time thinking about validity and soundness.

In order for an argument to be valid, it must follow a proper deductive form. But, what exactly does that mean? Compare the following two valid deductive arguments concerning Jerry. Compare...

Premise 1: All comedians tell jokes.
Premise 2: Jerry is a comedian.
Therefore,
Conclusion: Jerry tells jokes.

to

Premise 1: All readers of Superman Comics have superpowers.
Premise 2: Jerry is a reader of Superman comics.
Therefore,
Conclusion: Therefore, Jerry has superpowers.

You might notice that both arguments share the same logical structure or form. The form is the following, using the letters A, B, and C as variables, or places holders.

Premise 1: All A's are B's.
Premise 2: C is an A.
Therefore,

Conclusion: C is a B.

Put just slightly differently,

Premise 1: Everything in category A is also in category B.

Premise 2: C is in category A.

Therefore,

Conclusion: C is also in category B.

In our initial argument concerning Jerry being a comedian, "category A" refers to comedians, "category B" refers joke-tellers, and "C" refers to Jerry himself. In our subsequent argument concerning Jerry having superpowers, "category A" refers to readers of Superman Comics, "category B" refers to those who have superpowers, and "C" again refers to Jerry himself. Both arguments are valid. However, only the argument concerning Jerry (Seinfeld) being a comedian is also sound. The argument concerning Jerry having superpowers is valid but not sound. The following argument form is also valid.

Premise 1: All A's are B's.

Premise 2: C is not a B.

Therefore,

Conclusion: C is not an A.

For any way we fill in variables here, if the premises are true, the conclusion will be true as well. Here's an example that seems to illustrate this point.

Premise 1: All chemists are scientists.

Premise 2: Jesse is not a scientist.

Therefore,

Conclusion: Jesse is not a chemist.

So, we now have two examples of valid deductive arguments:

Premise 1: All A's are B's.

Premise 2: C is an A.

Therefore,

Conclusion: C is a B.

Premise 1: All A's are B's.

Premise 2: C is not a B.

Therefore,

Conclusion: C is an A.

What would an invalid argument form be? Remember, if an argument is invalid, that means that it is not *really* a deductive argument. In other words, if an argument form is invalid, that means that it would be possible for the premises to be true and the conclusion to be false. Consider the following argument form.

Premise 1: All A's are B's.

Premise 2: C is a B.

Therefore,

Conclusion: C is an A.

This is an invalid form. How do we know? What proves that it is invalid is the fact that we can come up with at least one example where we fill in the

variables such that the premises are true and the conclusion is false. If it were valid, that would be impossible. Here is one such example.

Premise 1: All dogs are mammals.

Premise 2: Garfield (the cat) is a mammal.

Therefore,

Conclusion: Garfield (the cat) is a dog.

In this example "dog" is a stand in for A, "mammal" is a stand in for B, and Garfield is a stand in for C. This one example shows that the form in question is invalid. Both premises are true, but the conclusion is false. That said, it's worth pointing out that even if we could fill in the variables such that the premises were true *and* the conclusion were true, that wouldn't make it valid. From the fact that we have this one example where the premises are true and the conclusion is false, that shows that the entire argument form is invalid.

Here's one more example of an invalid argument form.

Premise 1: All A's are B's.
Premise 2: C is not an A.
Therefore,
Conclusion: C is not a B.

And, here's an instance of this argument form that shows that it is invalid.

Premise 1: All dogs are mammals.
Premise 2: Garfield (the cat) is not a dog.
Therefore,
Conclusion: Garfield (the cat) is not a mammal.

Again in this example, "dog" is a stand in for A, "mammal" is a stand in for B, and Garfield is a stand in for C. Both of the premises are true, but the conclusion is false. So, the whole form is invalid. Remember, if this were a valid argument form, it would be impossible for us to come up with an example where the premises are true but the conclusion is false.

So, thus far we've seen two valid argument forms and two invalid argument forms.

Valid:

Premise 1: All A's are B's.

Premise 2: C is an A.

Therefore,

Conclusion: C is a B.

Valid:

Premise 1: All A's are B's.

Premise 2: C is not a B.

Therefore,

Conclusion: C is an A.

Invalid:

Premise 1: All A's are B's.

Premise 2: C is a B.

Therefore,

Conclusion: C is an A.

Invalid:

Premise 1: All A's are B's.

Premise 2: C is not an A.

Therefore,

Conclusion: C is not a B.

Exercise 1.5

For each of the following argument forms, provide an example according to the direction provided. Remember, for each example A should represent a category of things, B should represent at category of things, and C should represent a particular thing.

1. The following argument form is *invalid*. Provide an example with one true premise, one false premise, and a true conclusion.

Premise 1: All A's are B's.

Premise 2: C is a B.

Therefore,

Conclusion: C is an A.

2. The following argument form is *valid*. Provide an example with two false premises and a true conclusion.

Premise 1: All A's are B's.
Premise 2: C is an A.
Therefore,
Conclusion: C is a B.

3. The following argument form is *invalid*. Provide an example with two true premises and a true conclusion.

Premise 1: All A's are B's.
Premise 2: C is not an A.
Therefore,
Conclusion: C is not a B.

4. The following argument form is *valid*. Provide an example with two true premises and a true conclusion.

Premise 1: All A's are B's.
Premise 2: C is not a B.
Therefore,
Conclusion: C is not an A.

5. The following argument form is *invalid*. Provide an example with one true premise, one false premise, and a false conclusion.

Premise 1: All A's are B's.
Premise 2: C is a B.
Therefore,
Conclusion: C is an A.

6. The following argument form is *valid*. Provide an example with two false premises and a false conclusion.

> Premise 1: All A's are B's.
> Premise 2: C is an A.
> *Therefore,*
> Conclusion: C is a B.

7. The following argument form is *invalid*. Provide an example with two true premises and a false conclusion.

> Premise 1: All A's are B's.
> Premise 2: C is not an A.
> *Therefore,*
> Conclusion: C is not a B.

8. The following argument form is *valid*. Provide an example with one true premise, one false premise, and a true conclusion.

> Premise 1: All A's are B's.
> Premise 2: C is not a B.
> *Therefore,*
> Conclusion: C is not an A.

9. The following argument form is *invalid*. Provide an example with two true premises and a true conclusion.

Premise 1: All A's are B's.

Premise 2: C is a B.

Therefore,

Conclusion: C is an A.

10. The following argument form is *valid*. Provide an example with two false premises and a false conclusion.

Premise 1: All A's are B's.

Premise 2: C is an A.

Therefore,

Conclusion: C is a B.

11. The following argument form is *invalid*. Provide an example with one false premise, one true premise, and a false conclusion.

Premise 1: All A's are B's.

Premise 2: C is not an A.

Therefore,

Conclusion: C is not a B.

12. The following argument form is *valid*. Provide an example with one true premise, one false premise, and a false conclusion.

Premise 1: All A's are B's.

Premise 2: C is not a B.

Therefore,

Conclusion: C is not an A.

Exercise 1.6

The following argument form is invalid. What would prove that it is invalid? If you can, provide that proof (briefly explain your answer).

Premise 1: All A's are B's.

Premise 2: C is a B.

Therefore,

Conclusion: C is an A.

CHAPTER 2
Logic and Language

Chapter 2

Logic and Language

As we learned in Chapter 1, logic is the study of arguments. That said, no logic text would be complete without also saying something about language as well. The reason for this is that if we are not careful with our use of language in the arguments we employ and evaluate, then the value of logic will be reduced to the value of a game like Sudoku or of a Rubik's Cube. Our investigation of logic will give us fun puzzles to solve, but it won't help us in our search for the truth. Consider the following argument.

Premise 1: All fill-in-the-blanks are shmill-in-the-blanks.

Premise 2: Patchy is not a shmill-in-the-blank.

Therefore,

Conclusion: Patchy is not a fill-in-the-blank.

Is this a valid argument? Yes, it is. It follows a proper deductive form. If the premises are true, the conclusion would have to be true as well. The argument follows the following form which you may recognize from Chapter 1.

Premise 1: All A's are B's.

Premise 2: C is not a B.

Therefore,

Conclusion: C is not an A.

The argument is valid. Is it sound? Is there any way to know that? What is a fill-in-the-blank? What is a shmill-in-the-blank? *Who (or what) is Patchy*?! The point is this. If we aren't clear in regard to what we are talking about, if we have no concern for the precision of the language that we use, we might be able to determine whether or not an argument is *valid*, but we won't be able to determine whether or not the conclusion of an argument is actually supported by its premises; we'll have no idea if an argument is sound.

If we care about the truth, we have to think carefully about language, because that is how we communicate the truth as we see it. If we care about rationality, we have to think carefully about language, because language is the vehicle through which rationality is delivered.

Literal and Figurative Language

Suppose it's raining so hard that you'd only need to stand outside for a few moments to get absolutely drenched. Under circumstances such as these, consider the following two claims.

> 1. It is *not* raining.
>
> 2. It is raining cats and dogs.

Here are what seem to be two obvious points that we could make about these claims. Both claims are *in some sense* false. Under the circumstances described "It is not raining." is straightforwardly or *literally false*. And of course, "It is raining cats and dogs." is false in the sense that it is *not literally true*. Cats and dogs have never (in my experience) rained down from the sky in the same way that water often enough does.

That said, even with that in mind, "It is raining cats and dogs." would typically be *treated* as if it is true. It would be odd (and perhaps irritating) if someone were to respond to the claim "It is raining dogs." with "That's not true." or "What are you talking about? *Raining cats and dogs*? It never rains cats and dogs!"

The straightforward reason for this is that "It's raining cats and dogs." – though this claim itself is not *literally* true – is a fairly obvious stand-in for a claim that *is* literally true: something like "It is raining really hard." And, it is quite common (and arguably very useful) to occasionally employ figurative language in order to color our words with metaphor or allegory. And, it is this point that can help us articulate the difference between literal and figurative language. To use **literal language** is to use terms in their most typical or basic sense *without* the use of metaphor or allegory. To use **figurative language** is to use terms in a way that goes beyond their most typical or basic sense by using metaphor or allegory.

We know "It's raining cats and dogs." is not literally true, but it paints a linguistic, metaphorical picture that gets our mind onto the idea that *is* literally true, that it is raining really hard. And, this is the point. Figurative claims (e.g. "It is raining cats and dogs.", "She's as cold as ice.", "The sea was angry that day my friends.") *themselves* are not literally true; a figurative claim is true insofar as it corresponds to a claim that is literally true. The figurative claim "It is raining cats and dogs." is true insofar as it corresponds to the literally true claim "It is raining really hard."

It's important that we think carefully about the distinction between figurative and literal language. If we want to communicate understanding and be careful about the inferences that we make and the beliefs that we form, sometimes using figurative language is useful; other times it is not.

In the early 2000's, Major League Baseball was embroiled in a steroids scandal. A number of prominent players had been using steroids and in so doing, had broken a handful of long-standing, cherished records. The use of steroids had not been *explicitly* banned by the rules of Major League Baseball, but many (if not most) surrounding the game believed that it was nevertheless an underhanded, fraudulent practice that was tantamount to cheating. Because of this moral (or lawful) ambiguity, it was not uncommon during this time for commentators of the game to raise the question "Is the steroid scandal in baseball really just a witch hunt?" It was also not uncommon for this question to be debated almost endlessly among those surrounding the game at all levels (e.g. sports writers, fans, players, themselves, etc.). Perhaps unsurprisingly, these conversations rarely got anywhere and were almost always left unresolved. Why? One could argue it was because of the way in which the question itself was asked: "Is the steroids scandal in baseball really just a witch hunt?" Well, those who expressed concerns about the use of steroids in baseball were not on a *literal* witch hunt. They were not *literally* hunting for witches.

The problem with employing figurative language (in this way) in a debate (such as this) is that the claim in question that "The steroid scandal in baseball *is* just a witch hunt." lends itself to a wide number of varied, incompatible interpretations much more than any piece of literal language would. If two people unknowingly interpret "witch hunt" differently, and then try to have a debate about whether or not the steroid scandal in baseball is just a witch hunt, they are likely to just talk past one another and make no headway toward resolving their disagreement. Anyone wanting to have a dialogue about the worthiness or value of investigating steroids in baseball and potentially punishing users should be more careful about the language that they use to raise the question.

This is not an isolated case. Consider claims like "Money can buy happiness." or "Beauty is in the eye of the beholder." We could debate the truth of these claims seemingly *unendingly*. This is almost certainly (in part) because these are figurative claims which are wide open to varied, incompatible interpretations. It certainly isn't *literally* true that money can buy happiness. No one can *literally* buy happiness in the same way that a person can literally buy (for example) pencils or cheeseburgers. There is no happiness *store*. So, before we debate whether or not "Money can buy happiness.", it would almost certainly be a time-saver to first determine what is meant by the claim. That is, what is the literal claim which corresponds to the figurative claim "Money can buy happiness."? Similarly, when one claims "Beauty is in the eye of the beholder.", they almost certainly do not mean to suggest that there is literally some object that we will call "beauty", and it can be found if we dissect the eyeball of some person known as "the beholder". Thus, before we debate whether "Beauty is in the eye of the beholder" we should first get clear on what it means. What is the literal claim which corresponds to the figurative claim "Beauty is in the eye of the beholder."?

Exercise 2.1

Each of the following claims contains a piece of figurative language. As best you can, rewrite each claim using no figurative language. When possible, have your literal translation contain the same level of vividness as the original, figurative claim.

Example:

"It's raining cats and dogs."

Acceptable Answer:

"It's raining really hard."

Better Answer:

"The current rate of rainfall is so high that it is hard to see or maneuver outside."

1. "After her embarrassing Tweet, Cheryl's phone started to blow up."

2. "You've been told a million times: clean up your room!"

3. "Bill thinks that his Intro to Logic class is a big joke."

4. "The sea was angry that day my friends, like an old man trying to send back soup in a deli!"[59]

5. "Beauty is in the eye of the beholder."

6. "I'm heading to Las Vegas in a few days, and I've got some money that's burning a hole in my pocket."

7. "She's as cold as ice."[60]

---

59 Seinfeld and David (1994).
60 Jones and Gramm (1977).

8. "Bill and Fran enjoyed watching the sunset."

9. "When you sign up for classes, it's important not to bite off more than you can chew."

10. "Love is blind."

11. "Before you judge him, you should try to walk a mile in his shoes."

12. "Money can buy happiness."

13. "We can't wait here any longer for this client; time is money!"

14. "Careful buddy, you're on thin ice!"

15. "The pen is mightier than the sword."

16. "Don't count your chickens before they hatch."

17. "I was able to kill two birds with one stone."

18. "No man is an island."

19. "No one likes sore loser."

20. "She believes it deep within her heart."

Literal and Figurative (and Evolving) Language

Language evolves. If you are reading this book you are (at least in some sense) an English speaker which is a language that has been around for somewhere between 1,400 – 1,500 years.[61] However, if you were to travel back in time to try to have a conversation with some of the first English speakers, or if you were to travel back to the halfway point between the birth of the English language and the time you are reading this book right now to try to have a conversation with *those* English speakers, you would have a very rough time communicating with either group. Not only would the vocabulary and the rules of grammar be different, but the meaning of certain words would be slightly or completely different.

One example of a word with an evolved meaning over time is the word "brilliant". The literal meaning of "brilliant" (in American English) *today* is something like "extremely or especially intelligent". However, this was not always the case. Originally, this use of the term was figurative. The original literal use of the term was something like "sparkling or shiny". And of course, it is not difficult to recognize the intended metaphor. When something is sparkling or shiny it stands out and is easily noticed. And, when someone is highly or especially intelligent, they too (in perhaps a different way) stand out and are easily noticed. However, it would seem as if the (original) figurative use of "brilliant" was used so frequently that over time it became the literal use of the term.

---

61 Baugh (2012).

The distinction between literal and figurative language is easy to understand in the abstract, but potentially difficult to apply in particular circumstances. At one time the literal use of "brilliant" expressed "sparkling". Today, the literal use expresses "especially intelligent". This seems to imply that there was a long stretch of time where the literal meaning of "brilliant" was not fixed, or it was a matter of dispute. And, this highlights an important point about the nature of the distinction between literal and figurative language: there are a number of cases in which it is ambiguous or unclear whether or not a term is being used as a piece of figurative language. Consider the case of the term "fuel" or "fueled" along with the following uses of the term.

1. "The pickup truck is *fueled* by diesel gasoline."

2. The fire was *fueled* by the starter-log.

3. The energy-bar *fueled* the athlete's workout.

4. The couple's love affair was *fueled* by their shared love of bird-watching.

For any two uses of the term "fueled", is the term being used in the exact same way, in a completely different way, or in a way such that there is a metaphorical link between the two uses? For uses 1 and 2, it seems as if the term is being used (more or less) in the exact same way. For uses 1 and 4, it seems as if the term is being used (at best) in a way that has some sort of metaphorical link. Perhaps "fueled" is used literally in 1 but figuratively in 4. But, how about 1 and 3? Are they used in the exact same way or in a way such that there is merely a metaphorical link between the two? It may not be completely obvious. To be sure, both uses express a type of chemical process which allows a system to access potential energy. However, the processes may be different enough so that we think that there is merely a metaphorical link between the two uses of "fueled". The point is that the meaning of our terms, including the relationship between them is not always 100% clear and can sometimes be a matter of reasonable disagreement. Language (in general) and the meaning of our terms (in particular) are not fixed; these things are not written down somewhere in an authoritative text, never to be questioned. On the contrary, we should be mindful of the fact that language evolves and that there *can be* varied uses of a single term with no obviously "correct" use of the term.

Exercise 2.2

One italicized word is used in each set of sentences below. Consider the use of the word in both instances. For each pair, answer the following question. Is the word used (more or less) the same in both instances, is the use of the word completely different in each instance, or is there some sort of metaphorical link between the two uses? Give a brief explanation for your answer.

Example:

a. "1968 Ford Mustang for sale - $5,000; *firm*."

b. "Arnold is doing crunches because he wants a *firm* stomach."

Answer:

Metaphorical Link

Explanation:

The use of "firm" in the first instance means something like "not willing to accept a lower price". The use of "firm" in the second instance means something like "physically hard". In this sense, they are very different. However, there still seems to be a relevant similarity between them in that for both instances, (either in terms of price or in terms of muscles) the use of "firm" means "unmovable" (albeit in a relevantly different way).

1.   a. "That shirt will *shrink* if you run it through the warm wash cycle."

         b. "My *shrink* says I have some real issues to work out with my mother."

2.   a. "I think I failed by geometry *test* today."

         b. "I took my car to the mechanic to *test* the battery."

3.   a. "It's my *party*, and I'll cry if I want to (cry if I want to)."[62]

         b. "Will the Gore *party* please come forward? Your table is ready."

4.   a. "NBC News was the first to *break* the story."

         b. "You can't make an omelet, if you don't *break* some eggs."

5.   a. "1968 Ford Mustang for sale - $5,000, *firm*."

         b. "We're pleased that you've decided to join our law *firm*."

---

62 Gold (1963).

6.   a. "If your car breaks down, try to *flag* down another motorist."

       b. "The principal raises the *flag* at the beginning of each school day."

7.   a. "If he starts throwing punches, be sure to *duck*."

       b. "Ralphie and his family enjoyed *duck* for Christmas dinner."

8.   a. "If your car breaks down, try to *flag* down another motorist."

       b. "The anti-virus software will *flag* any problems with your laptop."

9.   a. "The egg is about to *hatch*."

       b. "Lex Luther knows how to *hatch* a plan."

10.   a. "The *date* of the meeting is Nov. 6th."

        b. "Sam has a hot *date* tonight."

11.   a. "Suzy is a popular gal, she has *dates* scheduled for every Saturday this month."

        b. "These cookies are terrible; did you put *dates* in the them?"

12.   a. "I think Bill and Fran are a good *match*; they should date."

        b. "Striped pants and a plaid shirt? Those don't *match* at all!"

13.　　a. "Dr. Van Nostrand has to perform *heart* surgery this afternoon."

　　　　b. "Rudy showed a lot of *heart* out on the field today."

14.　　a. "The judge's ruling was just and *fair*."

　　　　b. "Dr. Simpson is a *fair* grader."

15.　　a. "The school board's policy to cut funding to athletics was not *fair*."

　　　　b. "Mildred showed off her prize winning sow, Bessy at the county *fair*."

16.　　a. "Sorry, I can't stay; I have to *jet*."

　　　　b. "In the 1950's, it was a novelty to be able to travel by *jet*."

17.　　a. "Amazon is looking to *corner* the market on essentially all retail."

　　　　b. "The best place for the bookshelf is in the *corner* of the room."

18.　　a. "It's fairly tedious to have to hear about someone else's drug *trip*."

　　　　b. "Don took Betty on a *trip* to Rome.

19.　　a. "Could you pick up a *pound* of beef at the grocery?"

　　　　b. "Ivan Drago is really going to *pound* Rocky when they fight."

20.　　a. "I dropped Medieval Literature 101, because I lost *interest* in it."

　　　　b. "You should invest your money to accumulate *interest*."

21.   a. Sam to Dianne: "My dearest, how I *long* for you."

       b. "How *long* is the line for Metallica tickets?"

22.   a. "I need something *heavy*; bring me that anvil."

       b. "We covered some pretty *heavy* topics in my philosophy class"

23.   a. "If you want to get strong, you have to lift *heavy* weights."

       b. "Metallica is probably my favorite *heavy* metal band right now."

24.   a. "I can draw a perfect 90° *angle* freehand.

       b. "He's really trying to *angle* his way into the conversation."

25.   a. "The earth completes one *revolution* around the sun each year."

       b. "The writings of John Locke played an important role in the American *revolution*."

Categorization

One of the most basic skills that intelligent creatures (e.g. human beings) display is the ability to put things into categories. And of course, this is also an important and useful skill. We categorize things like tigers and steep cliffs as hazards or things to be avoided. And, we categorize things like wheat or puppies as things that are non-hazards or things to be enjoyed. To be sure, there is no one correct way to categorize any particular group of things. Whether or not it is useful to do so, everything in the universe can be classified as either a giraffe or a non-giraffe.[63] That said, there are at least a few guidelines to consider when categorizing a group of things. First, we'll consider a few (potentially familiar) definitions.

A **genus** is a broad category of things. A **species** is a more narrow category or a subcategory of things. And, a **referent** is a particular thing. So, we might consider the genus: U.S. landmarks. We could then subdivide U.S. landmarks into two species: natural U.S. landmarks and man-made U.S. landmarks. A referent that would then fall under the species of man-made U.S. landmarks would be the St. Louis Arch. We may visualize the categorization in the following manner.

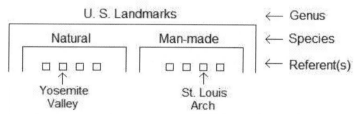

Similarly, we might consider the genus: baseball players. We could then subdivide baseball players into three species: pitchers, position players, and designated hitters. A referent that would then fall under the species of position players would be Ozzie Smith, a (former) shortstop for the St. Louis Cardinals. We may visualize the categorization in the following manner.

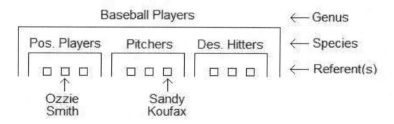

---

63 Thanks for this example to Dr. David Ciochhi.

Now, the point is this. While it *may* be the case that there is no perfect or objectively correct way to categorize what we find in the world, some categorizations are better than others.

A good categorization should meet (at minimum) two standards. The categorization should be mutually exclusive and jointly exhaustive. A categorization is **mutually exclusive** if and only if no referent can be put into more than one species. A categorization is **jointly exhaustive** if every referent can be put into at least one species.

Here is an example of a categorization that is not mutually exclusive.

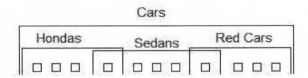

Of course, there is at least one thing (i.e. one referent) that is both a sedan and a Honda. Honda makes a number of sedans. Also, there is at least one thing that is both a red car and a sedan There are plenty of red sedans on the road today. Because of these reasons, this categorization is not mutually exclusive. We might say that this fails the test of mutual exclusivity.

Here is an example of a categorization that is not jointly exhaustive.

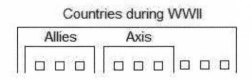

Not every country was on the Allied or Axis side during Word War II (e.g. Switzerland and Portugal were officially neutral during the war). So, this categorization is not jointly exhaustive.[64] We might say that this categorization fails to meet the standard of being jointly exhaustive.

Exercise 2.3

For each of the following classifications, ask the following two questions: is the categorization mutually exclusive? And, is the categorization jointly exhaustive? If the answer is no to either of these questions, give a clear counterexample that demonstrates that the categorization is either not mutually exclusive or not jointly exhaustive (and explain your answer). *If the categorization is both mutually exclusive and jointly exhaustive*, then answer the question (as best you can), how useful is the categorization (or, in what context might the categorization be useful)?

Example: U.S. Senators: Republican, Democrat.

Answer: This categorization is not jointly exhaustive because there are U.S. Senators who are registered Independents.

Example: Guitars: electric, acoustic, vintage, bass.

---

64 Of course, it is possible for a categorization to fail to meet both the standards of being mutually exclusive and being jointly exhaustive. The example involving cars (e.g. Hondas, red cars, sedans) is just such as an example since there is also at least one car that can be placed under none of those species (e.g. a blue Ford hatchback).

Answer: This categorization is not mutually exclusive because there are guitars that are both acoustic and vintage (and, there are guitars that are both electric and bass, vintage and electric, etc.).

Example: Bicycles: those ridden by Elvis Presley at least once, those never ridden by Elvis Presley.

Answer: This categorization is both mutually exclusive and jointly exhaustive. But, it is difficult to see how (or in what context) it would be useful (with maybe the possible exception of Elvis Presley memorabilia collecting).

1. Songs: rap, rock n' roll, #1 hits, sung by Bjork.

2. Pants: on sale at the Gap, corduroy, leather, khaki.

3. Basketball Players: those who have successfully dunked a basketball on a regulation rim (at least once), those who have not successfully dunked a basketball on a regulation rim (at least once).

4. College Courses: Humanities, Fine-Arts, Social-Science, Hard-Science, Other Science, Engineering, Physical Education, Career & Technical, Mathematics, Business.

5. Sports: those that use a ball, team, water, Winter.

6. U.S. States: coastal, land-locked.

7. Baseball teams: professional, semi-professional, amateur.

8. Movies: Academy Award winning, thriller, western, buddy-cop, those starring Ethan Hawke.

9. Schools: public, private.

10. Land on Earth: private, public.

11. Football players: defensive players, offensive players.

12. Telephones: mobile, landline.

13: Foods: dairy, processed, junk-food, meat, vegetables.

14. Jefferson College students: those who are 6' tall and shorter, those who are > 6' tall.

15. Religions: monotheistic, non-monotheistic.

16. Books: paperback, non-fiction, re-released.

17. Undergraduate students: freshman, sophomore, junior, senior.

18. Computers: desktops, laptops.

19. Apartments: studios, 1 bedroom, 2 bedroom, 3+ bedroom.

20. Businesses: Tourism, Food-Service, Railroads, Sales, Hospitals, Manufacturing, Air-travel.[65]

Defining Terms

A key skill in the use of logic is being able to deliver clear and precise definitions for important terms. We can't merely rely on dictionaries for this, because that is not the purpose of a dictionary. The purpose of a dictionary is to give someone a very basic, elementary understanding of what a term means, if they previously had no idea what is meant by the term. In both your thinking and your writing, you will often want something more clear and precise than the type of definition that a dictionary can offer. As a general (though perhaps not universal) rule, you should never use a dictionary definition in your (college level or professional) writing. For instance, if you are writing a paper for an ethics class on capital punishment, no part of your paper should include

---

65 Daniels (2007).

"Webster's Dictionary defines 'Capital Punishment' as...." Again, this is because a dictionary is not intended to give you the clarity and precision you most likely want in your writing and thinking. It is intended to give someone a rough understanding of the common usage of words day-to-day. And, in your college level and professional writing, you can assume that your reader has at least a very basic, elementary understanding of what (terms and phrases such as) "Capital Punishment" mean(s).

At any rate, having clear, precise definitions is a vital part of the study and use of logic. If (for instance) you were engaged in a debate of the merit of religion in society, it would prove helpful to have *at least* a working, rough definition of "religion". Likewise, if we were considering the morality of euthanasia, it would likely be important to have *at least* a working, rough definition of "euthanasia". If we don't define our terms, we risk talking past one another, making no progress in our conversation or thought.

With that in mind, it will benefit us to spend at least a bit of time thinking critically about how best to do this. The type of definition we'll focus on here is definition by genus and differentia. As we previously mentioned, a **genus** is a broad category of things. A **differentia** is a set of distinguishing characteristics. So, when giving a definition by genus and differentia, it should take (roughly) the following form.

Term/Concept = Genus + Differentia.

For instance, if we wanted to define the term "laundry", we might do so in the following manner.

Laundry is clothing that is going through the wash cycle.

Here, the genus of our definition is "clothing" while the differentia is "going through the wash cycle". How about the concept of a "mailman"?

A mailman is a person who works for the U.S.P.S.

Here, the genus is "person", while the differentia is "works for the U.S.P.S."

With this in mind, here are six rules (or guidelines) to keep in mind when defining a term.

Rule #1: A definition should contain both a genus and a differentia.

This rule might seem obvious seeing as we are attempting to give definitions *by genus and differentia*. But, it is still worth mentioning. Consider the following definition.

A race is when two people try to see who's the fastest.

This definition has no genus. "When" is not a genus; it is not a category of things. A better, more precise definition might be...

A race is a contest in which two parties determine who can span a given distance in the shortest interval of time.

In contrast to our initial definition, this definition *does* have a genus - "contest" – which is a category of things.

Here's another example.

A grilled-cheese is a sandwich.

This definition has no differentia. It is true that a grilled-cheese is a sandwich, and that is likely the best genus for us to choose to define the term, but without a differentia, our definition is incomplete. A better, more precise definition might be something like the following.

A Grilled-Cheese is a sandwich toasted with cheese in some form of fat such as butter or margarine.

"Toasted with cheese in some form of fat such as butter or margarine" is our differentia and gives us a clearer, more precise definition than our original example.

The specifics of these examples aren't as important as is the general lesson that in order to deliver a clear, precise definition, make sure it includes both a genus and a differentia.

Rule #2: A definition should include the "essential at tributes" of the term or concept being defined.

The "essential attributes" of a concept are the properties of that concept that make the concept *what it is*. Consider the following example.

A guitar is a musical instrument made popular in the middle of the 20ᵗʰ century by the emergence of rock 'n roll.

It is of course a historical fact that the guitar was made popular in the middle of the 20ᵗʰ century because of rock 'n roll, but that's not what makes a guitar what it is. That's not what makes a guitar a *guitar*. A better definition might be something like the following.

A guitar is a musical instrument with a fretted fingerboard played by plucking or strumming its strings.

That a guitar has strings, that it has a fretted fingerboard, and that it is played by plucking or strumming are (collectively) closer to the "essential attributes" of a guitar. It is those properties which make a guitar what it is. Again, while our initial example might be an interesting fact *about* guitars. Our second example is certainly a better *definition* of "guitar".

Here's another example.

A burrito is a Mexican dish that can be purchased at *Chipotle*.

Much like the previous example, this definition does not get at the essential attributes of the concept in question. Of course, it is true that burritos can be purchased at *Chipotle*, but that's not what makes a burrito a burrito. If there were no *Chipotle* restaurants, there would still be burritos. A better definition might be something like the following.

A burrito is a Mexican dish which consists of a tortilla rolled around fillings such as meat, vegetables, and cheese.

These are the elements that make a burrito what it is – these are the "essential attributes" of the concept of a burrito.

Rule #3: A definition should be neither too broad, nor too narrow.

This rule might be the most important rule of the ones covered here in that if your definition does not violate this rule in any way, it is unlikely (though not impossible) that you will have violated the other rules on the list. What does it mean for a definition too be too broad? What does it mean for a definition to be too narrow? A definition is too broad if it includes things that it shouldn't. A definition is too narrow if it excludes things that it shouldn't. Consider the following example.

A bird is an animal that flies.

This definition is *both* too broad *and* too narrow. There are animals which don't fly that are birds such as penguins and ostriches. These examples demonstrate that the definition is too narrow, because the definition excludes them when it should not. And, there are animals which do fly that are not birds such as mosquitoes and bats. These examples demonstrate that the definition is too broad, because the definition includes them when it should not.

Consider the two definitions we surveyed earlier in the chapter.

Laundry is clothing that is going through the wash cycle.

and...

A mailman is a person who works for the U.S.P.S.

Are these definitions too broad? Too narrow? Arguably, things like towels and sheets are laundry. Since the proposed definition of "laundry" excludes those items as being laundry, it is too narrow.

How about the definition for "mailman". The person who works behind the counter, processing the mail is someone who works for the U.S.P.S., as is the person who designs the stamps. Yet, those people probably wouldn't be considered to be mailmen – even though they fit the criteria for the definition in question. So, the proposed definition for "mailman" is too broad.

The point here is that a definition can be subject of two different types of *counterexamples*. If you can find a counterexample of a definition including something that it shouldn't, the definition is too broad. If you can find a counterexample of a definition excluding something that it shouldn't then the definition is too narrow.

Rule #4: A definition should avoid ambiguous, flowery, and figurative language.

Poetry is an important art form. Metaphor is a useful and (in the right context) can provide a deeper level of insight that we wouldn't be able to achieve without it. However, in providing a definition for a term, these uses of language should be avoided. The purpose of a definition is to communicate understanding though clarity and precision. So, you want to avoid language in your definition that is widely open to varying interpretations (in the way that flowery or figurative language can be). Consider the following example.

"I define love thus: The will to extend oneself, for the purpose of nurturing one's own or another's spiritual growth."

- M. *Scott* Pech, The Road Less Traveled[66]

While there is a certain level of depth through the imagery here, this quote may fall short of the goals that we've outlined above for offering a definition. Here is a different definition which captures this same sentiment but also achieves the goals of clarity and precision a bit better.

Love is a state of being in which one genuinely desires the good of (and union with) another person or being.[66]

Of course, the correct definition of a complicated concept such as love is (and may always be) a matter of philosophical dispute. But, if one were to attempt to define such a concept, this is the *type* of a definition that one would want to give, as opposed to a definition which employs flowery or figurative language.

---

66 On this topic, see: Stump (2012).

Rule #5: A definition should not be circular.

A definition is circular if there is a term in the definition that would be meaningless or unknowable without the term that is being defined. Remember, the purpose of a definition is to communicate understanding through clarity and precision. A definition which contains terms that are meaningless or unknowable without the term that one is trying to define certainly cannot accomplish this task. Here is a definition which fails this test.

Fraud is knowingly and willfully attempting to defraud another person or party.

To be sure, the term "defraud" is meaningless or unknowable without the term which this definition attempts to define, "fraud". Perhaps a better definition would be something like the following.

Fraud is the act of knowingly and willfully deceiving another person for one's own personal gain that deprives the deceived of their moral or legal rights.

In order to avoid constructing a circular definition, you should avoid using root words in your definition (e.g. "science" shouldn't be defined using the word "scientists", etc.). However, this is not the only way in which a definition may be circular. If a definition contains a word that is essentially interchangeable with the word being defined (e.g. "freedom" and "liberty"), that may also constitute a circular definition. In any particular case, in order to determine whether or not a definition is circular, we should ultimately appeal to the purpose for giving a definition: communicating understanding through clarity and precision. If a definition does not accomplish this task because a term in the definition is too closely related to the term we are trying to define, it may be circular (in a way that we want to avoid).

Rule #6: A definition should not use a negative term (e.g. "not") unnecessarily.

There are certain terms that cannot be defined without a negative. The negative is built into the concept itself. For instance, the term "atheism" is typically defined as "the view that God does *not* exist." There is no getting around using a negative term in the definition of atheism; that is what "atheism" *means*. Similarly "darkness" might be defined as the *absence* of light. That's what darkness *is*. The point behind rule #6 is that with the goal of avoiding making your definition unnecessarily complicated, you should not include a negative term when you do not need one. Consider the following example.

A capitalist is one who rejects communism, socialism, or any other economic system in which the state has a primary control over the market or trade.

The term "capitalist" needn't be defined simply in terms of what a capitalist is not (e.g. a communist, socialist, etc.). A better definition might be something like the following.

A capitalist is one who defends the claim that one's income should be directly tied to his or her ability to provide goods and services which others are willing to freely exchange their resources in order to obtain.

Most definitions (though certainly not all) do not require a negative term such as "not", "without", or "absence". So, if your definition contains such a negative term, make sure that it does not break rule #6.

Exercise 2.4

Each of the following definitions breaks at least one of the rules for defining terms covered in the previous section. For each example, identify the rule that is broken. Then, offer a brief explanation of how the definition breaks that rule. In some cases, a definition may break more than one rule. When this occurs, pick out and focus on the rule that is broken the most flagrantly.

Example:

A sport is a competitive activity that is played with a ball.

Answer:

Rule Broken: Rule #3: A definition should neither be too broad, nor too narrow.

Explanation: This definition for "sport" is too narrow, because it excludes sports such as hockey (which uses a puck, instead of a ball) and wrestling (which uses no ball nor any ball-like object).

Example:

A theory is an idea which exists entirely in the realm of the theoretical and has not yet entered into the realm of the factual.

Answer:

Rule Broken: Rule #5: A definition should not be circular.

Explanation: This definition for "theory" contains the word "theoretical", which is a term that would be meaningless or unknowable without the term "theory".

1. A lion is a jungle cat which is native to Africa.

2. A theist is someone who is neither an atheist nor an agnostic.

3. "Hypocrisy is the homage that vice pays to virtue."

- Francois La Rochefoucauld, *Maxims and Reflections*

3.5 To believe something is to act as if it is true.

4. Happiness means getting what you want.

5. An airplane is a vehicle which was invented by the Wright Brothers in 1903 in Kitty Hawk, NC.

6. "Life is the art of drawing sufficient conclusions for insufficient premises."[67]

- Samuel Butler, *Notebooks*

7. A cause is an event which produces an effect.

8. A government is a human organization which imposes rules on people.

9. Honesty is the habitual absence of the intent to deceive.

10. Deception is the act of intentionally and successfully deceiving some other person.

11. "Torture is any act by which severe pain or suffering, whether physical or mental, is intentionally inflicted on a person for such purposes as obtaining from him or a third person information or a confession."[68]

- United Nations Convention Against Torture

12. Health is the absence of any injury, disease, or any other harmful medical condition.

13. Patience means waiting.

---

67 Butler (2016).
68 United Nations (1985).

14. A movie is a visual form of entertainment which became widespread in the U.S. and Europe in the late 19th and early 20th centuries.

15. Faith is the human capacity for a soul to travel beyond what is allowed by their firm foundation into harmony with another.

16. An army is the branch of a country's military which uses tanks.

17. A radio is a frequency receiving device that can be found in most automobiles.

18. To hate something is to treat it with disdain.

19. "Freedom of choice: the human capacity to choose freely between two or more genuine alternative or possibilities, such choosing being always limited both by the past and by the circumstances of the immediate present."

- Corliss Lamont, *Freedom of Choice Affirmed*[69]

20. Murder is the act of intentionally ending the life of another human being.

21. Lying is the act of saying something false.

22. An organic substance is any substance that is not inorganic.

23. "Alteration is combination opposed determinations in the existence of one and the same thing."

- Immanuel Kant, *Critique of Pure Reason*

24. "To sneeze is to emit wind audibly from the nose."

- Samuel Johnson, *Dictionary*[69]

25. A computer is a calculating device.

26. A computer is a device which provides us with seemingly unlimited access to information via the internet.

27. A politician is a person who makes his or her living fulfilling some elected or appointed role within the political realm.

28. "To explain is to strip reality of the appearances, covering it like a veil, in order to see the bare reality itself."

- Pierre Duhem, *The Aim and Structure of Physical Theory*

29. A raincoat is an outer garment of rubber which repels water.

30. Intelligence is the human trait which an I.Q. test attempts to measure.

---

69 Johnson (1814).

31. "Love means never having to say you're sorry."

- Erich Segal, *Love Story*

32. Love is the tacit understanding between two like-minded souls that all that this world has to give is not enough for true harmony amongst them.

33. The mind is that which takes part in mental events or states of being.

34. Wine is an alcoholic beverage made from grapes.

35. "Frankness is saying whatever is in our minds."

- Richard C. Cabot, *The Meaning of Right and Good*[70]

36. A map is a piece of paper containing a visual representation of a physical space.

37. "By analysis, we mean analyzing the contradictions in things."

- Mao Zedong[71]

38. An expert is any individual which has the innate ability, relative to some sub-field or sub-discipline, to employ his or her expertise in regards to said sub-field or sub-discipline.

---

70 Cabot (2010).
71 Zedong (1957).

39. A game is a competitive human activity which is governed by rules.

40. A quinceañera is when a girl from Latin American turns 15 and throws a big party.

41. Protestantism is the branch of Christianity which is a collection of churches that is not governed (or overseen by) either by the Roman Catholic Church or the Eastern Orthodox Church.

42. A vest is a piece of clothing which does not have sleeves.

43.. "Home is a place where, when you have to go there, they have to take you in."

- Robert Frost, The Death of a Hired Man[72].

44. "Knowledge is true opinion."

- Plato, Theaetetus[73]

45. A crime is an action that is punished by some governmental authority in a court of law.

46. "War is an act of violence intended to compel our opponent to fulfill our will."

- Carl Von Clausewitze, On War

---

72 Frost (1914).
73 Plato (1990).

47. "Art is the human activity having for its purpose the transmission to others of the highest and best feelings to which men have risen."

- Leo Tolstoy, *What is Art?*[74]

48. To be gullible is to have the ability to be fooled.

49. "Life is what happens when you're busy making other plans."

- John Lennon, *Beautiful Boy*[75]

50. A drug is any substance which (when exposed to the blood or digestive tract of the human body) brings about a chemical change to the body.

---

74 Tolstoy (2013).
75 Lennon (1980).

CHAPTER 3
Fallacies

Chapter 3

Fallacies

This chapter is about fallacies. A **fallacy** is a flaw or an error in reasoning. Put differently, a fallacy has been committed when someone uses an argument in a way that is mistaken. The use of a fallacy doesn't necessarily mean that someone has arrived at a false conclusion. After all, like anything else in life, it is at least possible to make a mistake and still arrive at success. You can make a wrong turn and (perhaps through a series of fortunate events) still arrive at your destination. You can forget to carry the one, pick the wrong stock, and still make a profit in the market. And of course, you can commit a fallacy and nevertheless end up at the truth. That said, logic (much like life in general) is about mitigating risk. And, avoiding fallacies is a way of mitigating risk. While committing a fallacy doesn't necessarily entail that you will end up with a false belief, it certainly raises the chance that you will. So, because we are concerned with believing truths and avoiding believing falsehoods, we'll want to pay special attention to fallacies: what they are and how we can avoid them.

When someone commits a particularly egregious fallacy, it (at times) is not too hard to notice. Consider the following conversation.

> Salesman: "I highly recommend this tiger repellent spray. It's on sale for only $500 a bottle!"
> Potential Client: "Well, I'm not sure I'm in the market for that sort of thing. But, how do I even know if it works?"
> Salesman: "Well, I just sprayed it all over, and you don't see any tigers around, do you?!"

This, of course, is a bad argument. It's an argument that employs fallacious reasoning. Just because there are no tigers around after the (so called) tiger repellent has been employed, that does not prove (and may not even provide much evidence whatsoever) that the tiger repellent actually repels tigers.

Chances are, that's not a groundbreaking revelation to you. You didn't need to be told that the Salesman's pitch was (let's say) dubious. In fact, there are likely a number of examples in this chapter that you will immediately recognize as flawed or dubious reasoning. In those cases, you don't need to learn or to be told that you are being presented a fallacious argument. The benefit then of studying such examples is to begin to recognized *patterns* of mistaken reasoning and to give a name to such patterns. Developing this ability will then come in handy when you are confronted with a dubious argument with a mistake that is less than immediately obvious (and perhaps, when the stakes are much higher than they are currently).

Formal Fallacies

In deductive logic, a **formal** (as opposed to an informal) **fallacy** is an invalid argument. It can be thought of as an argument which is presented as a deductive argument even though it is possible for the premises to be true and the conclusion to be false. This is sometimes known as a *non sequitur* which literally means "It does not follow."

One common formal fallacy is known as "affirming the consequent" and it has the following form.

> Premise 1: If P, then Q.
> Premise 2: Q.
> *Therefore,*
> Conclusion: P.

A conditional claim (in the case, Premise 1) is made up of an antecedent and a consequent. In this case the antecedent is P. The consequent is Q. Premise 2 is an affirmation of the consequent, Q (i.e. Premise 2 is just the claim that Q is true). So, that is why we call this (invalid) argument form "affirming the consequent".

There may be many cases in which we could fill in the variables (i.e. P and Q) such that the premises are true and the conclusion is true. However, you may recall from Chapter 1, all that it takes to prove that this is an invalid argument (or a formal fallacy) is one example in which we fill in the variables such that the premises are true, and the conclusion is false. Here is one such example.

> Premise 1: If Mick Jagger was a member of the Beatles, then Mick Jagger has been in a rock n' roll band.
> Premise 2: Mick Jagger has been in a rock n' roll band.
> *Therefore*,
> Conclusion: Mick Jagger was a member of the Beatles.

As he was the lead singer of The Rolling Stones, Mick Jagger has in fact been in a rock n' roll band. And of course, it is true that if Mick Jagger was a member of the Beatles, the Mick Jagger has been in a rock n' roll band. However, it is not the case that Mick Jagger was a member of the Beatles. So, this one example demonstrates that "affirming the consequent" is invalid. It is a formal fallacy.

Another common formal fallacy is known as "denying the antecedent" and it has the following form.

> Premise 1: If P, then Q.
> Premise 2: It is not the case that P.
> *Therefore*,
> Conclusion: It is not the case that Q.

Again, Premise 1 is a conditional. Premise 2 is a denial of the antecedent (i.e. P). In other words, Premise 2 is the claim that P is false (and therefore, 'it not the case that P' is true). That is why we call this (invalid) argument form "denying the antecedent".

Again, as with any formal fallacy, all that we need to show that an argument form is invalid is one example in which we fill in the variables such that the premises are true but the conclusion is false. Here is one such example of "denying the antecedent".

> Premise 1: If Michael Jordan was a wide receiver for the Chicago Bears, then Micheal Jordan was a professional athlete.
> Premise 2: It is not the case that Michael Jordan was a wide receiver for the Chicago Bears.
> *Therefore*,
> Conclusion: It is not the case that Michael Jordan was a professional athlete.

Michael Jordan never stepped on an NFL field as an NFL player (for the Chicago Bears or any other team). And of course, it is true that if Michael Jordan was a wide receiver for the Chicago Bears, then Michael Jordan was a professional athlete. However, Michael Jordan – one of the greatest NBA players of all time – was in fact a professional athlete (so, 'It is not the case that Michael Jordan was a professional athlete.' is false). So, this one example demonstrates that "denying the antecedent" is invalid. It is a formal fallacy.

There are many more formal fallacies we could here list. In fact, the number of formal fallacies has no end. However, for the remainder of this chapter, we will focus our attention on informal fallacies.

Informal Fallacies

We said in the previous section that a formal fallacy was an invalid argument. It is an argument that is presented as deductive even though it is possible for the premises to be true and the conclusion to be false. An **informal fallac**y then is an error in reasoning that is not an invalid argument but has a common flawed assumption or otherwise employs some other flawed reasoning strategy.

In what follows, we will list and describe a number of (unfortunately) common informal fallacies. It's worth pointing out that this is not an exhaustive list – no such list exists. Alas, human beings are continually coming up with new and innovative ways to reason poorly.

> **Ad Hominem**: an *ad hominem* occurs when someone attacks an arguer instead of (or when they should be attacking) an argument.

The fallacy of *ad hominem* might be the most familiar informal fallacy on our list. The phrase itself literally means "to the person". When someone attempts to reason that an idea is false or that an argument should be rejected on the basis of the existence of some sort of flaw in the person expressing the idea or making the argument, they are committing an *ad hominem*. Consider the following example.

> Senator Ross has argued that we need to raise the minimum wage to keep pace with inflation and to help out (so called) struggling families. But Senator Ross is a career politician who has never run his own business. He has no clue about how this will affect the economy; he simply doesn't know what he is talking about, and his proposal should be summarily rejected.

If a person is claiming to be an expert in some area, and on that basis asks us to accept his testimony *as an expert*, then a lack of relevant experience is certainly something that needs to be taken into consideration. However, this is not the case in this example. The proposal in question should be accepted or rejected based on the strength of the ideas and arguments of the proposal itself and not on the basis of the person who happens to be expressing those ideas or making those arguments.

Of course not all *ad hominem* arguments are this blatant; they can be much more subtle. Consider the following example.

Of course your pastor would say that it's perfectly rational to believe in God, his job depends on people believing in God!

Simply because someone might have a vested interested in people believing their claims or being persuaded by their arguments, that in itself is not a good reason to believe that what they are claiming is false. Examples such as this in which someone attacks a person making an argument solely on the basis that there may be some sort of material bias are sometimes called *circumstantial ad hominem* attacks.

Ad hominems, are certainly a fallacy we should strive to avoid, but it is worth pointing out that not all attacks on one's character constitute an instance of an *ad hominem*. Such an attack is only a fallacy when it is done *in place of an argument*. For instance, if someone points out that a presidential candidate has a long track record of dishonest business dealings or a lack of executive leadership experience, that is not necessarily an *ad hominem* attack. When we elect politicians, we are not merely electing a set of ideas, but a flesh and blood person whose character may be extremely important to consider. That said, as we saw in our initial example, if someone attacks another person's character and presents that as some sort of evidence that their ideas are false or that their arguments are flawed, that is fallacious reasoning.

Appeal to Popularity: an appeal to popularity occurs when it is argued that something is true simply because a large number of people believe it to be true.

Sometimes called "Appeal to the People" or "Appeal to the Majority"[76], the appeal to popularity fallacy is fairly straightforward. The fact that a large group of people all believe that something is true is not *itself* a particularly strong reason to believe that thing. So, if a person argues that something is (likely) true simply on the basis that a large or significant number of people believe that it is true, that person is committing the fallacy of appeal to popularity. Consider the following example.

It's estimated that somewhere around 80 million Americans today believe in astrology. With that many people on board, they have to be on to something. Count me in![77]

Interestingly, there are perhaps some cases which may be thought of as exceptions to the rule when it comes to appeal to popularity. For instance, if there are multiple *independent* eyewitness to some event, their testimony can serve as fairly strong evidence that the event in question did in fact occur as they say it did.[78] That said, aside from these unique, very specific cases, the fact that a large number of people believe that something is true itself provides hardly any reason whatsoever to conclude that it is in fact true.

Appeal to Inappropriate Authority: an appeal to inappropriate authority occurs when someone believes or argues that something is true based on the testimony of a non-expert.

---

76 Additional names for this fallacy are the bandwagon fallacy, common belief fallacy, argument from consensus, mob appeal, and *argumentum ad populum*.
77 This is in fact a well researched statistic. See: Gecewicz (2018).
78 Joyce (2019).

It is a simple fact of life that we must – on occasion – rely on the testimony of experts to help us navigate the world. And, if done so correctly, relying on the testimony of experts does not involve making any sort of logical or rational mistake. If after a close and thorough examination, your physician tells you that you have the measles, that's a fairly good reason to conclude that you do in fact that the measles. However, if your childhood friend from down the street takes a quick glance at your arm and says "Oh yeah, that's the measles alright, my sister had it real bad a couple of years ago.", that is probably not a terribly good reason to conclude that you have the measles.

This example may be fairly straightforward to the point that it might seem that it could go unsaid. However, it invites us to think carefully about the concept of expertise and the length to which it can be stretched. A competent, experienced physician should count as an expert in regard to diagnosing ailments such as the measles. But, if your physician tells you "I'm a doctor, trained in the science of medicine. I assure you, life does not begin at conception."[79], that is not a great reason to conclude that "life" does not begin at conception (or at any other point in human development). The concept of "life" in the sense that we use it to argue about (for instance) abortion is a philosophical concept that can't be decided by medical science alone.

Similarly, if an academically trained cosmologist told you some interesting fact about black holes, it could very well be rational to believe that fact simply on the testimony of the cosmologist. However, if the cosmologist explained to you his theory about extraterrestrial life and how they have visited this planet, this likely falls outside of the bounds of his expertise and it would likely be reasonable to remain skeptical on the issue.

False dichotomy: the fallacy of false dichotomy occurs when one concludes that something is true based on a set of assumptions

---

79 And of course, if a physician tried to argue on the basis of his medical expertise that "life" *does* begin at conception, he would be committing the same fallacy.

that erroneously limits the options that are in fact available.

Sometimes called "False Dilemma", "False Choice", or "The Black and White Fallacy", the fallacy of false dichotomy occurs when there is in fact a greater number of choices than what is presented when some sort of (theoretical or practical) decision is to be made. Here is one such example.

In a free-market, capitalist society, there are the winners and the losers. And I can tell you, the game is rigged against you. You have no legitimate shot at being one of the winners!

The issues with capitalism not withstanding, this is a fallacious piece of reasoning. For the sake of argument, suppose that a free market system does produce "winners" and "losers". The fabulously wealthy can be considered winners of the system. Those living in abject poverty are the losers of the system. But of course, "winner" and "loser" are simply too broad as categories to describe every person in such a system. Consider the person who works 45 to 50 hours a week at a difficult job, but can afford a comfortable home, a yearly vacation, and to retire at a reasonable age. Is that person a "winner" or a "loser"? What seems more reasonable is that the argument in question if flawed (as it is a false dichotomy), because we need additional categories to describe the economic realities and outcomes of those who participate in a free market economy.

Sunk Cost Fallacy: the fallacy of sunk costs occurs when one makes a cost/benefit calculation about the rationality of some potential future action but in so doing, factors in a previously invested resources which cannot be recovered.

The fallacy of sunk costs is something that most of us have been (or will be) guilty of at some point in our lives. It's hard to admit mistakes. It's not easy to move on from the past. But, if you're not careful, this will lead you to fallacious reasoning (which could literally cost you). Imagine you've spent hundreds of dollars on your car just to get it to pass inspection. Then, your mechanic informs you that you'll need to spend another $1,000 because you need a new rotary girder (and without it, your car won't run). You are trying to decide whether to pay for the new part or to put that money towards a new car (that may be more reliable). You might be tempted to think...

Well, I've already put so much money into the car I already have. It would seem like a waste to just junk it and buy a new one.

But of course, this line of reasoning commits the sunk cost fallacy. The money that you've spent on your car already can be thought of as a "sunk cost". It is a resource that has already been spent and cannot be recovered. So, it would be a mistake to take it into account when figuring the utility of putting *new* money towards fixing your current car or purchasing a new one.

The sunk cost fallacy is not only committed when making purchases. Consider the following example.

Doris: "I really hate my boyfriend."
Mae: "Oh, yeah?"
Doris: "Yeah, he treats me bad."
Mae: "That's no good."
Doris: "And, I know he's cheating on me."
Mae: "Oof."
Doris: "And, to be honest, I just don't like being with him."

Mae: "So, why don't you break up with him already?!"

Doris: "Well, we've just been together so long!"

A sunk cost is a "resource" that cannot be recovered. But, a resource can be a number of different things. It can be money, but it can also be time, effort, emotional stress, etc.

Hasty Generalization: a hasty generalization occurs when one makes an inductive inference base on a(n inappropriately small) amount of evidence.

The fallacy of a hasty generalization is fairly straight forward. Making inductive inferences or inductive generalizations is unavoidable. A good number of your (arguably justified) beliefs are based on such generalizations. You believe that all (or nearly all) tigers have stripes. But how many tigers have you actually ever seen yourself? Do you believe that your logic instructor is a multi-millionaire? Why or why not?[80]

The point is this. While inductive generalizations are inevitable, they should not be made… hastily. They should only be made once a reasonable, sufficient amount of evidence has been collected. Consider the following example.

We had a Ford when I was growing up and it was always breaking down. My college roommate drove a Ford, and I always had to give him a ride, because it was so unreliable. My neighbor has a Ford and that thing is in the shop more than it's on the street. I'm sorry, but Fords as a whole are just terrible cars.

---

80 If your logic instructor is the author of this textbook, you can be assured that your logical instructor is not a multi-millionaire.

Millions upon millions of Fords have been sold over the past century. To infer something about Fords in general because of three anecdotal cases would be to commit the fallacy of hasty generalization.

Exercise 3.1

For each example, identify the fallacy that is being committed: *ad hominem*, appeal to popularity, appeal to inappropriate authority, false dichotomy, sunk cost fallacy, or hasty generalization. Be able to defend your answer.

Example: 70% of voters are convinced that President Muffley is corrupt and dishonest. I'm sorry; I simply refuse to vote for a liar, and we all better hope he doesn't get reelected.

Answer: appeal to popularity. The person making this argument is concluding that President Muffley is dishonest primarily (or entirely) on the basis that a large number of his fellow citizens have arrived at this conclusion. This is a clear case of an appeal to popularity.

1.   Nurse R. Ational: "… and for those reasons, I would argue that euthanasia is morally wrong."

Mr. S. Keptic: "Well of course you're going to say that; you're a hospice nurse. You wouldn't want to lose business!"

2. A company's CEO on a Zoom call from his mansion in the Malibu, California: "Look, we have a difficult but straightforward decision to make: either we lower wages for the employees, or we raise prices which will hurt sales."

3. Overly zealous Army General: "The leaders of Florin have said they refuse to

accept the terms of the deal under the current terms. Mr. President, our options now are to either blow them to smithereerns or to walk away from the negotiating table with our tail between our legs."

4. Ugh! This movie is the worst; I am so bored! I'd rather be doing literally anything else. Oh well, I'm an hour in. I might as well see how it ends.

5. Every time I've ever seen [insert random celebrity here] in an interview or out on the street with fans, she's always been so warm and cheery. It's nice to know that you can still be an overall good person even though you are rich and famous.

6. I'm not a doctor, but I play one on TV. Hi. I'm Neil Patrick Harris, and if you're dealing with a headache brought on by listening to your philosophy instructor drone on and on, you need fast-acting Provasic.

7. Professor Simpson has the highest class evaluations among the entire faculty in the math department. So, Professor Simpson must be the best, most effective instructor teaching College Algebra. You should definitely take it with him.

8. During the entirety of his campaign, Senator Che V. Ron assured his constituents again and again that (so called) climate change is a hoax. So, I can't for the life of me figure out why you still believe in it; there is just no such thing as "climate change".

9. As far as I know, the Jones family lives a fabulous, happy life. After all, in everything that I see them post on social media, they are all smiles and living their best life.

10. We all went to high school. You've got the jocks, the geeks, the skaters, the goths, the preppies, and last but not least: *the brainiac-nerds*. Troy is in AP Chemistry and AP Calculus. There's no way he's going to make the basketball team.

11. Team president to manager: "Look, we signed that veteran to a huge guaranteed contract. I don't care how bad he's playing, I'm not going to be spending all that money just to have him sit on the bench. For the last time, don't start that hot-shot rookie in his place anymore."

12. Why exactly are we studying the ideas of Freud? I mean, the guy was a cocaine addict for Pete's sake. What could we possibly learn from him? I'm sorry, but this just seems like a waste of time.

13. President Whitmore has argued for increased funding for NASA, SETI, and similar programs and organizations that might prepare us to one day meet intelligent, extraterrestrial life. But, Whitmore is just another pro-military conservative who is hoping to increase his power to surveil the American people.

14.   Jimmy: "[Being a lawyer] is not for me. I don't want it!"

       Kim: "Jimmy, do you remember how long you studied for [the bar exam]? How hard you worked? All that effort – you're just going to throw that away?!"[81]

15. Uh, has anyone even heard of *Cap'n Geech and the Shrimp Shack Shooters*? And they won album of the year?! Justin Bieber (or 'the Biebs' as I

81 Gilligan (2016).

114

like to call him) sold way more albums this year. He definitely should have won record of the year.

Exercise 3.2

Pick any two of the following fallacies: *ad hominem*, appeal to popularity, appeal to inappropriate authority, false dichotomy, sunk cost fallacy, or hasty generalization. Then, for both of the fallacies you have chosen, write a brief paragraph containing an argument that commits that fallacy. Remember, for the purposes of the exercise, you are trying to compose a bad argument. That said, try to make your example obvious enough to illustrate the fallacy being committed, but not so absurd that you could never imagine someone making that particular mistake.

Informal Fallacies (Continued)

Equivocation: The fallacy of equivocation occurs when one makes an argument containing the same word multiple times as if it has the same meaning in each instance though it in fact has different meanings.

The fallacy of equivocation is best understood by the use of examples. Consider the following.

The sign says "Fine for parking here." So, I parked there. The sign says it's fine!

The use of "fine" in the first instance means something like "financial penalty". The use of "fine" in the second instance means something like "permissible according to the rules". And, it is obviously fallacious to reason that it is "fine" (in the sense that it is permissible) to park in a particular spot, based on the fact that a sign reads: "Fine" (in the sense that there is a financial penalty) for parking in that spot.

Here's one more example.

> The first amendment says I have freedom of speech. Saying what is on my mind is my right. So, telling you that I think you are a big, dumb jerk whenever I feel like you are being a big dumb jerk is right.

The use of "right" in the first instance means something like "does not violate any law or common societal standard." The use of "right" in the second instance means something like "the moral thing to do, all things considered." Arguably, there are a great many things that are morally wrong even though we all have (in some sense) the "right" to do them. So, it would commit the fallacy of equivocation to reason that because you have the "right" to do something, that it is the morally "right" thing to do.

> **Appeal to Ignorance**: The fallacy of appeal to ignorance occurs when someone argues that something must be true simply because it hasn't been or can't be proven false (or *vice versa*).

Often, when the fallacy of appeal to ignorance is described, it comes with something of a tag line: the absence of evidence is not *necessarily* evidence of absence. Again, the fact that a claim hasn't been or can't be prove false is not itself a great reason to conclude that the claim in question is true. Conversely, the fact that a claim hasn't been or can't be proven true is not itself a great reason to conclude that the claim in question is false. Consider the following pair of examples.

No one has ever disproven the existence of extraterrestrial life (e.g. space aliens and what not). That's why I'm a firm believer in it!

There has never been any amount of truly substantial evidence to think that there exists life (intelligent or otherwise) other than on Earth. We are alone in the universe, and that's a fact!

Arguably, the assumptions of both of these arguments are plausible if not true. It has never been proven that space aliens exist. And, there has never been any truly substantial evidence (publicly available anyway) that would justify someone in believing that aliens exist.

However, both arguments make parallel mistakes in what is inferred from those starting assumptions. From the fact that alien life has not been proven to exist, it would be fallacious to conclude that it simply *doesn't* exist. And, from the fact that the existence of alien life has not been *disproven*, it does not follow that it does. The reasonable position is most likely to be agnostic on the matter (i.e. to take no position one way or the other).

Begging the Question: someone has "begged the question" when, in order to make their argument, they assume the very point at issue. Put differently, their conclusion can be found as one of their assumptions.

The phrase "begging the question" (or "begs the question") is often misused. People say "begs the question" when they really mean something like "raises the question". For example, someone might say "The starting quarterback was injured in practice. So, that begs the question, who is going to take the snaps on Sunday?" The fact that the starting quarterback was injured does not beg the question, it *raises* the question: who is going to start at quarterback the next game?

To beg the question is to assume the very point you are trying to reach with your argument. It is for one to make an argument with the conclusion already contained within the argument's premises. Suppose there has been a big heist at the art gallery. A ski mask was left at the scene of the crime and it's being admitted into evidence at the trial of the current number one suspect. The lawyer of the suspect (now defendant) might make the following (fallacious) argument.

> Your honor, we insist that the ski mask should not be entered into evidence. For you see, it is clear that the mask belongs to the thief. But, it's been our contention all along that our client is innocent; he isn't the thief. So, the mask has nothing to do with him. It's simply irrelevant.

The question the trial aims to resolve is whether or not the defendant is in fact the thief. And, the defense is trying to build the case that the defendant on trial isn't the thief. The defense can't have as an assumption that the defendant is not the thief to make the case that (the mask should not be entered into evidence in order to ultimately make the case that) the defendant is not the thief. To do so would be to argue fallaciously by begging the question.

> **Gambler's Fallacy**: a gambler's fallacy occurs when one reasons under the assumption that two independent events are somehow causally connected to one another.

The gambler's fallacy is sometimes called the Monte Carlo[82] fallacy. Both names are apt as it is not difficult to imagine a gambler at a casino

---

82 Monte Carlo is an area of Monaco which is known in part for its casinos.

118

thinking in this irrational manner.

> The last five spins on the roulette wheel were black. The next one's *gotta* be red!

The fact that the last five spins on the roulette wheel were black does not raise the probability that the next spin on the roulette wheel will come up red. The probability for each roulette spin to come up red is 47.4%[83] regardless of what the past spins were. This is because each spin on the roulette wheel is an independent event from every other spin. The odds of getting a series of six black spins in a row is astonishingly low. But, it is equal to the odds of getting five black spins in a row followed by a red spin.[84] The gambler in this example is considering a different question: given the fact that the last five spins were black, what are the chances that the next spin will be red? The answer is again: 47.4%.

As you might have guessed, the gambler's fallacy can be committed outside of a casino or gaming context. Suppose a wedding photographer is talking with a potential client, a nervous bride.

> Bride: "I'm so nervous; there are so many things that could go wrong. What if it rains?!"
>
> Photographer: "I don't think you have to worry about that. The last three weddings I booked all got rained on... *a lot*. That won't happen again. No one is that unlucky. Am I right?"
>
> Bride: *laughs nervously

---

83 This is for American roulette. In European roulette, the odds raise slightly to 48.6%.
84 In both cases, the chances are about 1.1%. In European roulette, the chances are about 1.3%

Presumably, there is no causal connection between days in which it rains and days in which weddings are scheduled. Just as in the roulette example, the

photographer here is committing the gambler's fallacy because he is treating independent events as somehow causally connected to one another.

Genetic Fallacy: a genetic fallacy occurs when one concludes that something must have a certain property simply because it had that property at its origin.

Things can and do change. Just because a person (or anything else) had a certain feature at its origin (or any other time), it does not follow that it has that feature currently. To reason that it does is to commit the genetic fallacy. Consider the following example.

The *Cosa Nostra* – or what is derisively called the "mafia" – began in Sicily to help fill a dangerous power vacuum and keep the peace as the country was transitioning from a feudal society to a capitalist one. So, what the authorities and Hollywood screenwriters call the mafia or the mob is really a good thing when you think about it.

While there is some truth to the assumption of this argument, it also commits the genetic fallacy. No matter how an organization (or anything else) begins, that does not say much about how it continues or its current state.

Here's an example of an argument that commits the genetic fallacy in a different way. Suppose you find out that a close friend has been accused of a terrible crime. You might initially think "There's no way they could possibly do that. I know them too well!" Motivated by this unfortunate turn of events, you dive head first into the case. You visit the scene of the crime, you interview eyewitnesses... you investigate the whole alleged incident like the most seasoned gumshoe. And, you really do come to learn that your friend really is innocent. As you lay out your case, someone might object...

Oh, c'mon! You only think that the accused is innocent because you're good friends with them. That's all there is to it!

However, this would commit the genetic fallacy. Even if your belief *originated* from your personal relationship – and your subjective sense that your good friend couldn't have committed such a crime – it does not follow that your belief *now* (since you have put in all of the investigative work) is not justified by solid evidence.

Of course, if you had not put in the work to study the case as you did, the accusation (or something similar enough) might stick, which brings us to the last fallacy on this list.

Appeal to Incredulity: an appeal to incredulity occurs when one concludes that a claim must be false simply because it seems fantastic or defies "common sense".

There are many things about the universe that are weird, counterintuitive, "unbelievable", but nevertheless true. The chair you're sitting in is mostly empty space. Under certain conditions, hot water will freeze faster than cold water. And, there are many more interesting facts that we could list here; the point is simply that things that *sound strange* are occasionally true. And, the fact that someone is particularly incredulous in regard to any particular claim does not constitute a solid reason (for that person or anyone else) to conclude that the claim is false. So, when someone makes an argument such as...

I just don't see how an ancient people like the Druids could have built a structure like Stonehenge. The whole thing seems a little too convenient if you ask me. There has to be more to the story. I'm thinking aliens.

... that person is committing the fallacy of appeal to incredulity.

Exercise 3.3

For each example, identify the fallacy that is being committed: equivocation, appeal to ignorance, begging the question, gambler's fallacy, genetic fallacy, or appeal to incredulity.

Example: Ugh, (first baseman Paul) Goldschmidt has been in a real slump lately. But that means he's due, right? I'm calling it now; He's going to hit a home run next time up.

Answer: gambler's fallacy. The person making this argument is suggesting that because Goldschmidt hasn't been doing well in recent at-bats, it is likely (or expected) that in his next at bat, he will be successful. However, each at-bat is an event that is independent from other at-bats. The person making this argument is treating them as if they are somehow causally connected.

1. The idea that we don't have free will – that all of our actions are predetermined – is just too hard a pill to swallow. The whole idea is just complete counterintuitive to me. So, it must be true that we have some sort of free will.

2. Whenever I travel on an airplane, I always make sure to bring an explosive

device with me. It just makes me feel more safe. After all, what are the chances there are going to be *two* bombs on the same plane?!

3. Jackasses have long ears. Carl is a jackass. Therefore, Carl has long ears.

4. I know for a fact that the employees think I'm a great boss and truly enjoy my meticulous, tough-but-fair managerial style. You see, in all my time on the job, I've never heard one complaint from any of them!

5. We know that the Bible is God's word because it says in II Timothy, Chapter three that all Scripture is divinely inspired from God.

6. We know that the Bible is not the "word of God", because we know that no supernatural being has ever delivered any sort of divinely inspired message to humanity.

7. You're trying to tell me that the movie *Rain Man*, was based on a true story? That there really was some guy on the spectrum who could just count cards and take loads of cash from casinos? Seems a little far-fetched to me; I don't buy it.

8. After the first day of Logic, I went straight to the registrar to drop the class. Dr. Heter went on-and-on about the fact that logic is the study of arguments. I get enough of that at home, my little brother and sister are getting in arguments morning, noon, and night. I don't need that sort of thing ruining my time at school too.

9. Of course Big Foot exists. There is not one single shred of evidence that he does not exist. The only reasonable conclusion to draw is that he does in fact

exist; don't listen to the naysayers.

10. Christmas has undeniable pagan roots. You see, when the Roman Empire was transitioning to and adopting Christianity, the powers that be thought it would be easier for the common folk if they converted the old pagan holiday of Saturnalia (celebrated towards the end of December) to the new "Christian"

holiday of Christmas. So, you can go to that Christmas Eve Mass if you want, just know that if you do, you are celebrating a pagan holiday.

11. I remember Davey from Little League. He couldn't throw, was slow as could be, and was scared of the ball when he was at the plate. There's no way he's going to make the varsity baseball team.

12. Nothing is better than tacos. A box of plain saltine crackers is better than nothing. Therefore, a box of plain saltine crackers is better than tacos.

13. When I moved to Springfield, I told my new neighbors that they don't have to worry about buying flood insurance. You see, I just moved from Shelbyville after their huge flood last year. And of course, the odds against one person experiencing two floods like that in two different towns two years in a row is astronomically small. I think we're safe.

14. When you really think about it, the set of tasks required for landing a man on the moon is truly mindboggling; I don't see how it could be done – even in principle. I just think it was all a hoax.

15. Prosecutor to a defendant who has plead not-guilty: "Tell us Ms. Kyle, what was it like to commit that terrible crime on the night in question?"

Exercise 3.4

Pick any two of the following fallacies: equivocation, appeal to ignorance, begging the question, gambler's fallacy, genetic fallacy, or appeal to incredulity. Then, for both of the fallacies you have chosen, write a brief paragraph containing an argument that commits that fallacy. Remember, for the purposes of the exercise, you are trying to compose a bad argument. That said, try to

make your example obvious enough to illustrate the fallacy being committed, but not so absurd that you could never imagine someone making that particular mistake.

Exercise 3.5

As in Exercise 3.1 and 3.3, for each example, identify the fallacy that is being committed: *ad hominem*, appeal to popularity, appeal to inappropriate authority, false dichotomy, sunk cost fallacy, hasty generalization, equivocation, appeal to ignorance, begging the question, gambler's fallacy, genetic fallacy, or appeal to incredulity. Be able to defend your answer.

1. If you don't support the President and his agenda, maybe you should just move to Canada, buddy!

2. Spokesman for *Aspirin-ExTREME*: "*Aspirin-ExTREME* relieves headaches fast. To put it simply, they make headaches go away! And, if you run a small business like I do, you know that doing your taxes at the end of the year can be a real headache. That's why I take *Aspirin-ExTREME*. They make my taxes go away!"

3. Of course *It's a Wonderful Life* is a bad film. After all, didn't you see how terrible it did at the box office? No one went to see that thing.

4. I'm completely stuffed. Every additional scoop of ice cream brings me no pleasure and is borderline painful. But, I've already paid for my dessert; I'm not going to just let it melt and go to waste.

5. Tim is trying to lay out the case that the defendant couldn't have committed the crime. He says that the DNA evidence exonerates him. But, Tim's just a kid. What does he know?

6. In Intro to Philosophy, Dr. Heter tried to argue for skepticism. He said that I could just be a brain in a vat hooked up to some supercomputer and that all my experiences are an elaborate illusion. But, I know that can't be true. I know that I'm sitting here in this room because of all of the things I can see, hear, and feel.

7. I remember you from way back in high school. You were shy – always stuck to yourself. You didn't have an ounce of charisma. I'm sorry, but I just can't have someone like that on my sales team. I can't offer you this job.

8. Imo's makes the best pizza, because no one makes a pizza better than they do.

9. Salesman for the *Home-Safety Defense System*: "Well sir, you are correct; I guess you don't *have to* purchase our product. I just thought you were interested in protecting your family from vicious criminals and evil-doers. I guess I was wrong about that."

10. My local, trusted newsman, Kent Brockman assured us that the migrating bees from Mexico aren't going to be a big problem. And, he's never steered me wrong on any other topic. I think we're going to be fine.

11. My Aunt Eunice smoked four packs of cigarettes a day for eighty years, and she lived to be ninety years old. So, I know smoking is perfectly safe.

12. I'm going to the Cubs game tonight; I just know they are going to win. They lost the last three games I went to. That can't happen to me four times in a row. Right?

13. No one has ever disproven the claims of astrology. That's why I check my horoscope everyday. There has to be something to it.

14. You're telling me that one lone gunman (from a book depository a great distance a way), this puny, insignificant man acted completely on his own and murdered the leader of the free world, John F. Kennedy? That just smells too fishy to me. There must have been a conspiracy.

15. Terence Mann is always saying that everyone must be willing to fight for what they believe in. But, he's also an avowed *pacifist*. If you ask me, he's just one big hypocrite.[85]

Exercise 3.6

Pick any three of the following fallacies: *ad hominem*, appeal to popularity, appeal to inappropriate authority, false dichotomy, sunk cost fallacy, hasty generalization, equivocation, appeal to ignorance, begging the question, gambler's fallacy, genetic fallacy, or appeal to incredulity. Then, for each fallacy you have chosen, write a brief paragraph containing an argument that commits that fallacy. Remember, for the purposes of the exercise, you are trying to compose a bad argument. That said, try to make your example obvious enough

---

85 Hint: this (fallacious) argument is also an enthymeme.

to illustrate the fallacy being committed but not so absurd that you could never imagine someone making that particular mistake.

Informal Fallacies for Further Consideration

As we mentioned at the top of this chapter, there is no exhaustive or complete list of informal fallacies. Even if there were, it would *become* incomplete soon enough as human beings are always finding new ways to argue poorly. So, the list of fallacies we've covered in this chapter is far smaller than list of fallacies you'll want to actively avoid using (or being persuaded by). With that in mind, here is a short, additional list of fallacies for you to consider and perhaps research on your own.

Straw Man: a straw man fallacy occurs when one responds to a distorted or particularly weak caricature of his opponent's argument, as opposed to his opponent's argument itself.

Red Herring: a red herring fallacy occurs when one diverts attention from the question at hand by raising a related but ultimately irrelevant issue.

Post-Hoc Fallacy: a *post-hoc* (*ergo propter hoc*) fallacy occurs when (for any two events: E_1 and E_2) one concludes that E_2 was caused or produced by E_1 simply because E_2 followed E_1.

Loki's Wager: the fallacy of Loki's wager occurs when it is argued that a meaningful conversation or debate cannot be had about a particular concept (or term) without a flawless definition of that concept (or term).

Fallacy of Composition: the fallacy of composition occurs when one argues that because a member of a group has a certain property, the group as a whole must have that property as well.

Fallacy of Division: the fallacy of division occurs when one argues that because a particular thing has a certain property, all of its parts must have that property as well.

Naturalistic Fallacy: the naturalistic fallacy occurs when one argues from purely descriptive premises to a normative (or value-laden) conclusion.

Slippery Slope: a slippery slope fallacy occurs when one argues – with little or dubious evidence – that a particular inciting event will set off a chain reaction, inevitably resulting in harmful or undesirable consequences.

No True Scotsman: a no true Scotsman fallacy occurs when one attempts to evade an objection to their universal generalization by excluding a potential counterexample in an *ad hoc* (or seemingly arbitrary) manner.

Exercise 3.7

After researching the fallacies found in the previous section, pick any three of the following fallacies: straw man, red herring, post-hoc fallacy, Loki's wager, fallacy of composition, fallacy of division, naturalistic fallacy, slippery slope, or no true Scotsman. Then, for each fallacy you have chosen, write a brief paragraph containing an argument that commits that fallacy. Remember, for the purposes of the exercise, you are trying to compose a bad argument. That said, try to make your example obvious enough to illustrate the fallacy being committed, but not so absurd that you could never imagine someone making that particular mistake.

CHAPTER 4
Semantics and Syntax

Chapter 4

Semantics and Syntax

Meaning and Structure

In previous chapters, we learned about deductive arguments. Recall that an argument is a deductive argument if and only if the truth of the premises guarantees the truth of the conclusion. In other words, if an argument is deductive, it would be impossible for the premises to be true and the conclusion to be false. Also, you may recall that there are two ways to evaluate deductive arguments: validity and soundness.

An argument is valid if and only if it follows a proper deductive form (and it is sound if it is valid and has all true premises), but how do we know whether or not an argument's form is actually deductive? In other words, how do we distinguish valid arguments from invalid arguments? Consider the following argument form.

> Premise 1: If P, then Q.
> Premise 2: P.
> *Therefore*,
> Conclusion: Q.

This is a proper deductive argument form (i.e. it is valid). But, how do we know that? It *could* be argued that we know this just by looking at the form or just by thinking about it. If Premise 1 is true, that P implies Q. And, if Premise 2 is true, if P is also true, then the conclusion, Q must be true as well. Here's an example that illustrates the point.

> Premise 1: If Walter is from Albuquerque, then Walter is from New Mexico.
> Premise 2: Walter is from Albuquerque.

Therefore,

Conclusion: Walter is from New Mexico.

When we fill in the details this way, it really does become clear that the argument is valid. If it really is true that Walter being from Albuquerque entails that Walter is also from New Mexico, and if it is true that Walter is from Albuquerque, then it *must* be true that Walter is from New Mexico.

So, at least in some cases, we don't have to do a ton of work to determine that an argument is valid. But, here's the problem. Even if it is true that we can potentially just "see" that an argument form is valid, this is an unreliable strategy for determining or recognizing the validity of arguments. If things get even just slightly more complicated, it won't be possible for us to just "see" that an argument form is valid. Because of this, we'll have to come up with a system for checking the validity of arguments.

The first step in developing a system to check the validity of arguments is to develop a language of formal syntax. We can distinguish between syntax and semantics. Think of the distinction this way. **Semantics** is the meaning of our everyday language (or of any meaningful sign or symbol whatsoever). **Syntax** is the logical structure of our language without the meaning; it is the way the semantics of or language is put together. Consider the claim "If the Mets lose, then Jerry will be sad." The semantics of this claim is just the meaning of the claim itself, that if it is true that the Mets lose, then it will be true that Jerry is sad. The syntax, or the logical structure of the claim is that it is a conditional claim or an "If-then" claim. Its logical structure is "If X, then Y." Likewise, consider the claim "Either George is marine biologist, or George is lying." The syntax, or the logical structure of this claim is that it is a disjunctive or an "either-or" claim. Its logical structure is "Either X, or Y." Think of syntax then as the part of a claim that would be left over if we ripped out all of the semantics. What would be left is just the logical structure of the claim.

Syntax Operators

Our formal syntax language will have two types of sentences: simple sentences and complex sentences. Simple sentences will be represented by capital letters A – Z. If we ever run out of letters (because we have more than 26 semantic claims that we need to "translate" into syntax) we can use subscripts (e.g. A_2, B_2, etc.). So, if we want to translate "Jerry dislikes Newman", we would just translate it as "J". We don't have to use J, we could use any upper case letter we wish, but it may be helpful for us to pick a key term in the sentence we are translating and use the first letter of that term. Consider how we might translate the following sentences.

- "Kramer loves to play golf." would simply be translated as K.
- "George is getting upset." would simply be translated as G.
- "These pretzels are making me thirsty." would simply be translated as P.

In contrast to simple sentences, complex sentences are made up of simple sentences and one of five "operators". An operator is a symbol or function that has an effect on the truth value of a sentence.

The first operator is a conditional. A **conditional** is an "if, then" claim. The symbol for a conditional is an arrow "→". So, if we wanted to translate the claim "If Jerry is a comedian, then Jerry tells jokes." we would translate it as "J → T" where J stands for "Jerry is a comedian and T stands for "Jerry tells jokes." Consider how we might translate the following sentences.

- "If George has a job with the Yankees, then George is employed." would simply be translated as G → E.
- "If Elaine loves David, then she will go to Arby's with him." would simply be simply be translated E → A.

- "If Tim is a dentist, then he went to dental school." would simply be translated T → D.

It's worth reminding ourselves that the capital letters represent sentences on their own: simple sentences. So, translating "If Jerry is a comedian, then Jerry tells jokes." as J → T, J doesn't stand for "Jerry"; J stands for "Jerry is a comedian". T doesn't stand for "tells"; it stands for "Jerry tells jokes". Translating "If George works for the Yankees, then George is employed." as G → E, G doesn't stand for "George"; G stands for "George works for the Yankees." E doesn't stand for "employed"; E stands for "George is employed."

The two parts of a conditional are called the antecedent and the consequent. The **antecedent** is the part of a conditional that comes directly after the "if". In the formal conditional 'X → Y', the antecedent is X. The **consequent** is the part of a conditional that comes directly after the "then". In the formal conditional 'X → Y', the consequent is Y.

The second operator is a **bi-conditional**. It's one thing to claim "If Newman comes to lunch, then Jerry will be upset." It's another thing to claim "If *and only if* Newman comes to lunch, then Jerry will be upset." This latter claim is likely untrue because any number of things could upset Jerry. The symbol for bi-conditional is a double arrow "↔". So, if we wanted to translate "If and only if Newman comes to lunch, then Jerry will be upset." we would translate it as "N ↔ U". Consider the following examples.

- "If and only if Kramer has free-time, then he'll play golf." would simply be translated K ↔ G.
- "If and only if Jerry is a comedian, then Jerry tells Jokes." would simply be translated J ↔ T.

The two parts of a bi-conditional are called the **components**. In the formal bi-conditional 'X ↔ Y', X is the left hand component; Y is the right hand component.

The third operator is a conjunction. A **conjunction** is an "and" or "but" claim. The symbol for a conjunction is an ampersand, "&". So, if we wanted to translate the claim "Jerry is a comedian, and George works in real estate.", we would translate it simply as "J & G". Consider the following examples.

- "Kramer is a neighbor, and Kramer is a doofus." would simply be translated K & D.
- "New York City is crowded, and Florida is hot." would simply be translated N & F.

The two parts of a conjunction are simply called the **conjuncts**. In the formal conjunction 'X & Y', X is the left hand conjunct, Y is the right hand conjunct.

The fourth operator is the a disjunction. A **disjunction** is an "Either, or" claim. The symbol for a disjunction is a carrot, "v". So, if we wanted to translate the claim "Jerry will either go the Mets game, or he will be annoyed.", we would translate it simply as "M v A". Consider the following examples.

- "Either Elaine marries JFK Jr., or Elaine will be sad." would simply be translated E v S.
- "Either George orders soup correctly, or George goes hungry." would simply be translated G v H.

The two parts of a disjunction are called the **disjuncts**. In the formal disjunction 'X v Y', X is the left hand disjunct. Y is the right hand disjunct.

Lastly, the fifth operator is a negation. A **negation** is a "not" claim or an "it is not the case" claim. The symbol for a negation is a dash, "−". So, if we wanted to translate the claim "Joe is not a nice person." (meaning "It is not the case that Joe is a nice person."), we would translate it simply as "– J". Consider the following examples.

- "Kramer is not a good neighbor." would simply be translated – K.
- "It is not the case that the New Jersey Devils won the hockey game." would simply be translated as – N.

Below is a summary of our five operators, the semantic language which picks out each of the of those five operators, the symbol used to represent those five operators, and the names of the parts of each of the complex sentences made up by the five operators.

Operator	Picked out by	Symbol	Names of parts
Conditional	"If, then"	→	antecedent/ consequent
Bi-conditional	"If and only if, then"	↔	components
Conjunction	"And", "But"	&	conjuncts
Disjunction	"Either, or"	v	disjuncts
Negation	"not"	–	N/A

We have to add one more piece to our syntax language before we can actually use it. We have to add parentheses. The reason is that our complex sentences can get more complex than the examples we've seen so far. Consider the following example.

"If George loses his job, then he'll have to go on unemployment, and he'll have to move back in with his parents."

What operators are contained in this sentence? Well, there is an "if-then" and there is an "and". So, it seems as if this sentence contains a conditional (i.e. a →) as well as a conjunction (i.e. a &). There are also three simple sentences in this complex sentence. "George loses his job.", "He'll have to go on unemployment.", and "He'll have to move back in with his parents." Presumably then, we would translate the example as follows.

G → U & P

The problem with this translation is that it is ambiguous. It could mean one of two things. It could mean either...

G → (U & P)

or

(G → U) & P.

The first potential translation would mean something like the following. "If George loses his job, then two things will follow: he'll have to go on unemployment, and he will also have to move back in with his parents." The second translation would mean something like "If George loses his job, then he'll have to go on unemployment, and then in independently of all that, it is also the case that he'll have to move back in with his parents." It seems fairly clear that the first translation is superior. So "If George loses his job, then he'll have to go on unemployment, and he'll have to move back in with his parents." should be translated "G → (U & P)".

Consider another example.

"If either David is at the hockey game, or David is at Arby's, then David is happy."

What operators does this sentence contain? There is a conditional, an "if-then" and a disjunction, an "either-or". And, there are three simple sentences: "David is at the hockey game.", "David is at Arby's", and "David is happy." The sentence seems to be indicating that if either one of two things occurs (i.e. David being at the Hockey game, or David being at Arby's), then a third thing will occur, David will be happy. Thus, "If either David is at the hockey game, or David is at Arby's, then David is happy." should be translated as follows.

(D v A) → H

D stands for "David is at the hockey game.", A stands for "David is at Arby's.", and H stands for "David is happy."

Here are a number of additional examples of complex sentences in which parentheses will have to be used.

- "If the Yankees do not win the World Series, and a team from New York does win the World Series, then the Mets win the World Series." Would be translated as (−Y & N) → M.

- "If and only if the Yankees do not win the World Series, and a team from New York does win the World Series, then the Mets win the World Series." Would be translated as $(-Y \& N) \leftrightarrow M$.

- "If either Kenny is at Jerry's apartment, or Newman is at Jerry's apartment, then Jerry will not be happy." would be translated as

$(K \lor N) \rightarrow -J$.

- "It is not the case that if Kramer is hungry then Jerry will feed him." would be translated as $-(K \rightarrow F)$.

Notes on Translating

Here are just a handful of things to keep in mind when translating form semantics to syntax.

1. Remember that each individual capital letter must represent its own simple sentence. If I wanted to translate "If Jerry is a comedian, then Jerry tells jokes." I might choose translate it as "J → T". "J" doesn't represent "Jerry"; "T" doesn't stand for "tells". "J" represents the sentence "Jerry is a comedian." "T" represents the sentence "Jerry tells jokes."

2. The only time an operator could start (or, come at the beginning of) a complex sentence is if it's a negation. These are all meaningful sentences (or, translations):

− C

− (P → Q)

− (P → Q) → (A v B)

These are all <u>incorrect</u> and <u>meaningless</u> sentences:

→ A v B

& (C → D)

↔ (P → Q) → (A v B)

3. The only time two operators can be "touching" or next to one another is when one is a negation (and it must come second). These are all meaningful sentences (or, translations).

A & − B

P → − Q

C v − D

These are all <u>incorrect</u> and <u>meaningless</u> sentences:

A − & B

P v → Q

X v ↔ Y

4. If a capital letter is used to represent one simple sentence, it should not be used to represent another simple sentence. If we wanted to translate "If Jerry is from New York City, then Jerry is from New York State." we might be tempted to translated it as "J → J". However, this would be incorrect because the first use of "J" represents the simple sentence "Jerry is from New York City."; we can't then use it to also represent the simple sentence "Jerry is from New York State." We should translate it as something like "J → N", "C → N", or even "X → Y".

5. Conversely, if a simple sentence does come up again, you must use the same capital letter to represent it. So, if we wanted to translate "Either Elaine has grace, or Elaine does not have grace." we would have to translate it as "E v − E", "G v − G", or even "X v − X".

Exercise 4.1

Translate the following examples from semantics to syntax.

Example:

If Logic is difficult, then Sally won't want to take it.

Answer:

L → − S

Example:

If and only if the children behave, then I will take them to the park and to get ice cream.

Answer:

C ↔ (P & I)

Example:

Either he's guilty, or he's not!

Answer:

G v – G

1. If the Vikings win, then Jefferson County will celebrate.

2. Either God exists, or God does not exist.

3. Today in my Introduction to Chemistry class, I learned the extremely interesting fact that the weight of a hydrogen atom is approximately one.

4. If you take Logic with Dr. Heter, then you will have wonderful mornings, and your life will be changed forever.

5. The test is Friday, and the quiz is Monday.

6. The test is Friday, and if you do not pass the test, then you will not pass the class.

7. If if Sam is from Springfield, then Tom is from Tuscon, then if Neil is from New York, then Bill is from Boston.[86]

8. If Jon is form St. Louis, then Jon is from Missouri.

9. It is not the case that it is not the case that it is not the case that *Buzzfeed* is a terrible waste of time.

---

86 No, there is no typo in this example.

10. "You got what I need, [and] you say he's just a friend."[87]

11. If the St. Louis Cardinal win the World Series, then Dr. Heter will be in a very good mood, and he will grade our tests much more charitably.

12. If and only if either it is 40 degrees below zero, or Dr. Booker is ill, then class will be canceled, and we can sleep in.

13. Either Logic class is not canceled, or I will cry.

14. If and only if either Logic class is not canceled, or I will cry, then if Logic class is canceled, then I will cry.

15. Just the other night I learned that the National College Athletic Association's College World Series is played each year in downtown Omaha, Nebraska at the very spacious *TD Ameritrade Ballpark*.

16. If either you are not a woman, or you are not not married, then you are not a bachelorette.

17. Saul is a dirty lawyer, but Jimmy is a nice guy.[88]

18. A hot dog is not a sandwich.

19. If you do not come to class, you will not pass.

20. The Professor of my Logic class, Dr. Joshua Heter told me that he grew up in the great city of St. Louis Missouri best known for being the home of the 11

---

87 Biz Markie, *The Biz Never Sleeps* (1989).
88 Remember, for our purposes, but = and.

time World Series Champion, the St. Louis Cardinals of the National League.

21. Either Logic is the best class at Jefferson College, or there is a class at Jefferson College that is better than Logic.

22. If you use 'than' when you should use 'then', then you need to brush up on your grammar.

23. If if and only if you have water, then you have H2O, then you water is identical to H2O.

24. If Dr. Heter can come up with anymore examples, then I would be surprised.

25. Dr. Heter does not have any more examples.

Exercise 4.2

Translate the following examples from semantics to syntax.

Example:

Sam is from San Antonio

Answer:

S

Example:

Sam is not from San Antonio

Answer:

– S

1. Bill is from Boston.

2. If Bill is from Boston, then Bill is from Massachusetts.

3. Either Bill is from Boston, or Bill is not from Boston.

4. It is not the case that Bill is from Boston, and Bill is not from Boston.

5. If Bill is from Boston, then Bill is from Massachusetts, and if Bill is not from Massachusetts, then Bill is not from Boston.

6. Either if Bill is from Boston, then Bill is from Massachusetts, or if Bill is not from Boston, then Bill is from somewhere else.

7. It is not the case that it is not the case that Bill is not from Boston.

8. Yesterday, when talking with my super friendly neighbor Betsy, I learned the extremely interesting fact that Bill is from Boston.

9. If and only if Bill is from Boston, then Bill is from Massachusetts, but not from any town that is not Boston.[89]

10. Bill is not from Boston.

11. It is not the case that Bill is not from Boston.

12. If Bill is not from Boston, then Bill cannot truly appreciate clam 'chowdah'.

13. If Bill is from Boston, then Bill is a Red Sox fan, and Bill isn't a Yankees fan.

---

89 Remember, for our purposes, but = can.

14. Bill is a fictional character who is purported to live in Boston created by Dr. Heter in order to construct a number of examples for the purposes of teaching his Logic students to translate semantic sentences into syntax sentences.

15. Bill is from Boston, and Betty is from Baltimore.

Exercise 4.3

Translate the following examples from semantics to syntax.

Example:

If the Cardinals won, then they scored more runs than the other team.

Answer:

$C \rightarrow S$

Example:

If and only if the Cardinals won, then they scored more runs than the other team.

Answer:

$C \leftrightarrow S$

1. The Cardinals won.

2. The Cardinals did not win.

3. Either the Cardinals won, or the Cardinals did not win.

4. If the Cardinals won, then the Cubs did not win.

5. If Wainwright is pitching, then the Cardinals win.

6. If and only if Wainwright is pitching, then the Cardinals win.

7. If the Cardinals win the game, then they will win the World Series, and Dr. Heter will cancel class.

8. If the Cardinals are playing the Cubs, then if the Cardinals win, then the Cubs will not win.

9. If either Stan or Red is up to bat, then it will either be a home run or a triple.

10. Today as I was waiting for the bus, I overheard the extremely interesting fact that the St. Louis Cardinals have won more World Series Championships than any other National League team.

11. If today as I was waiting for the bus, I overheard the extremely interesting fact that the St. Louis Cardinals have won more World Series Championships than any other National League team, then today was a good day.

12. Either the Cardinals will win, or the Cubs will win.

Exercise 4.4

Translate the following examples from semantics to syntax.

    Example:

    Luke is a Jedi.

    Answer:

    L

    Example:

Luke is a Jedi, and Han is a smuggler.

Answer:

L & H

1. Han is a smuggler.

2. Han is not a smuggler.

3. If Han is a smuggler, then Han is a scoundrel.

4. Either Han is a smuggler, or Han is not a smuggler.

5. Han is a smuggler, and either Luke is a Jedi, or Luke is not a Jedi.

6. If and only if Leia is a princess, then Leia is royalty.

7. Either Han is a Smuggler, or Luke is a Jedi.

8. If either Han is a Smuggler, or Luke is a Jedi, then Leia is a princess.

9. It is quite an interesting fact that Star Wars was released in 1977 to a great amount of fanfare.

10. Chewbacca is a Wookie.

Operators and Operations

Recall again our five operators: conditional, bi-conditional, conjunction, disjunction and negation. Or, as we have seen…

Operator	Picked out by	Symbol	Names of parts
Conditional	"If, then"	→	antecedent/ consequent
Bi-conditional	"If and only if, then"	↔	components
Conjunction	"And", "But"	&	conjuncts
Disjunction	"Either, or"	v	disjuncts
Negation	"not"	–	N/A

What's important for us to note here is that each operator has a "truth function". In other words, whether or not a complex sentence is true or false depends upon (at least in part) the function of the operators it contains. Think of truth functionality this way. There is a rule for each operator which determines when sentences containing those operators are true and false. Let's go over the five rules (corresponding to our five operators).

Conjunction: suppose during class one day, your logic instructor says "For our next class meeting, I will bring cookies, and I will bring milk." Under what set of circumstances would you consider this promise (or, this claim) false? Under what set of circumstances would you consider it true?

If the next class meeting, your instructor brings both cookies and milk, then what he said was true. However, if he only brings cookies, you might still be happy to enjoy the cookies (*sans* milk), but what he said was nevertheless technically false. If he brings milk, but not cookies, then you are much less

151

happy, and what he said was also false. And of course, if he brings nothing, then his claim "For our next class meeting, I will bring cookies and I will bring milk." is certainly false. So, here is the rule for conjunction: *a conjunction is only true when both conjuncts are true.*

If we translate the preceding cookies and milk claim as C & M, then we could visualize the rule in the following manner.

C	M	C & M
1. T	T	T
2. T	F	F
3. F	T	F
4. F	F	F

As you can see, only in the first line (when both C and M are true) is the conjunction "C & M" true. In every other instance, it is false.

What if instead of claiming "I will bring cookies, and I will bring milk." your instructor made the odd promise "Either I will bring cookies, or I will bring milk." Under what circumstances would this claim be true (or false)? To answer this, we must first make a distinction between an "inclusive or" and an "exclusive or". An **inclusive or** is a disjunctive claim (i.e. an either-or) claim which means "either one disjunct is true, or the other disjunct is true, or they are both true." An **exclusive or** is a disjunctive claim (i.e. an either-or) claim which means "either one disjunct is true, or the other disjunct is true, but it is not the case that both disjuncts are true." For our purposes of studying logic here, when we hear "or", or when we use the syntax symbol for it (i.e. the "v") we will be using the inclusive or.

So, if your instructor claims "Either I will bring cookies, or I will bring milk." and he bring both cookies and milk, what he said was true (again bearing

152

in mind that he is using the *inclusive* "or"). If he brings cookies, but he does not bring milk, what he said was true. If he does not bring cookies, but does bring milk, what he said was true. However, if he claimed "Either I will bring cookies, or I will bring milk.", he has said something false (only) if he brings neither. So, here is the rule for disjunction: *a disjunction is only false when both disjuncts are false.* We can visualize the rule in the following manner.

C	M	C v M
1. T	T	T
2. T	F	T
3. F	T	T
4. F	F	F

As you can see, only in the last line (when both C and M are false) is the conjunction "C v M" false. In every other instance, it is true.

Now suppose your instructor claims "If I bring cookies, then I will bring milk." Under what circumstances is this claim false? You might here ask, under what circumstances could you hold your instructor accountable for making a promise that he did not keep?

If he brings cookies, and he brings milk, then what he said was true. If he brings cookies, but does not bring milk, then what he said was false. But, if he brings no cookies but does bring milk, what he said was still true, or at least he can't be held accountable for saying something false. And, if he brings nothing, while you might be disappointed (having to go without either cookies or milk), what your instructor said was nevertheless true (or at least, you can't hold him accountable for having said something false). So, here is the rule for a conditional: *a conditional is only false when the antecedent is true and the consequent is false.* We can visualize the rule in the following manner.

C M	C → M
1. T T	T
2. T F	F
3. F T	T
4. F F	T

As you can see, only in the second line (when C is true and M is false) is the conditional, "C → M" false. In every other instance, it is true.

Now, suppose your instructor doesn't merely claim "If I bring cookies, then I will bring milk." Instead, your instructor claims "If *and only if* I bring cookies, then I will bring milk. This is obviously a similar but different claim. Under what circumstances would this more specific claim be true (or false)? Under what circumstances could you hold your instructor accountable for making a promise that he did not keep?

If your instructor brings cookies and brings milk, then what he said was true. And, if he brings nothing, what he said was technically still true (or at least, you couldn't hold him accountable for having said something false). But, if he brings cookies but does not bring milk, or if he brings milk but does not bring cookies, then what he said was false. So, here is the rule for a bi-conditional: *a bi-conditional is only true when both components are true, or both components are false*. We can visualize the rule in the following manner.

C M	C ↔ M
1. T T	T
2. T F	F
3. F T	F
4. F F	T

As you can see, only in the second and third lines is the bi-conditional "C ↔ M" false. In lines 1 and 4, it is true.

Our final operator to consider is the negation. And, it should not be difficult to imagine the truth conditions for a negation. If your instructor says that he will *not* bring cookies, but he does bring cookies, then (as much as you might not care) what he said was false. And, if he says that he will not bring cookies, and it false that he brings cookies, then what he said would be true. So here is the rule of the negation: *a negation is only false when the sentence being negated is true (and vice versa).* We can visualize the rule in the following manner.

C	– C
1. T	F
2. F	T

Here again our the five rules which correspond to the truth conditions for our five operators. It would almost certainly prove helpful if you commit these rules to memory.

1. Conjunction: A conjunction is only true when both conjuncts are true.

2. Disjunction: A disjunction is only false when both disjuncts are false.

3. Conditional: A conditional is only false when the antecedent is true and the consequent is false.

4. Bi-conditional: A bi-conditional is only true when both components are true and both components are false.

5. Negation: A negation is only false when the sentence being negated is true (and vice versa).

Exercise 4.5

Using the 5 rules (which correspond to the 5 different operators discussed in the previous section), determine whether the following claims are true, false, or unknowable. Put "T" if the claim is true; "F" if the claim is false; and "?" if there is not enough information to determine whether or not the claim is true or false. Remember, when you see blank spaces, you aren't attempting to fill in the blank, you are attempting (when possible) to determine whether the claim as a whole is true or false – even when you don't have all of the information. Be able to explain your answer.

Example:

(Jupiter is a planet) v _____.

Answer:

T

Explanation:

"Jupiter is a planet." is true, and it is a disjunct in a disjunction. A disjunction is only false when *both* disjuncts are false, so even though we don't know what the other disjunct is, we know that the claim (the disjunction as a whole) is true.

Example:

(The Sun is a planet) & _____.

Answer:

F

Explanation:

"The Sun is a planet." is false, and it is a conjunct in a conjunction. A conjunction is only true when both conjuncts are true, so even though we don't know what the other conjunct is, we know that the claim (the conjunction as a whole) is false.

Example:

_____ → (The Sun is a planet).

Answer:

?

Explanation.

"The Sun is a planet." is false, and it is the consequent of a conditional. A conditional is only false when the antecedent is true and the consequent is false. So, this conditional *could be* false, but in order to determine this, we would have to know what the antecedent is. If the antecedent is true, then the conditional would be false. If the antecedent is false, then the conditional would be true.

For the following examples, bear in mind the following information.

- The Cardinals are from St. Louis.
- The Cubs are from Chicago.
- The Yankees are from New York.
- The Royals are from Kansas City.

1. (The Cardinals are from St. Louis) v _____.

2. − (The Yankees are from New York) & _____.

3. _____ v (The Royals are from St. Louis).

4. _____ → (The Royals are from St. Louis).

5. – (The Cubs are from New York) → _____.

6. (The Royals are from Kansas City) ↔ (The Royals are from Kansas City).

7. – (The Royals are from Kansas City) ↔ – (The Cardinals are from St. Louis).

8. (_____ v – (The Cubs are from New York)) → _____.

9. ((The Yankees are from St. Louis) & _____) → _____.

10. ((The Yankees are from St. Louis) v _____) → _____.

11. _____ → (The Royals are from St. Louis).

12. _____ → (The Cardinals are from St. Louis).

13. _____ → – (The Cardinals are from St. Louis).

14. (_____ → _____) v (The Yankees are from New York).

15. (_____ → _____) & (The Cardinals are from St. Louis).

Exercise 4.6

Using the 5 rules (which correspond to the 5 different operators discussed in the previous section, determine whether the following claims are true, false, or unknowable. Put "T" if the claim is true; "F" if the claim is false; and "?" if there is not enough information to determine whether or not the claim is true or false. Remember, when you see blank spaces, you aren't attempting to fill in the blank, you are attempting (when possible) to determine whether the claim as a whole is true or false – even when you don't have all of the information. Be able to explain your answer.

Example:

_____ v (Venus is a planet).

Answer:

T

Explanation:

"Venus is a planet." is true, and it is a disjunct in a disjunction. A disjunction is only false when *both* disjuncts are false, so even though we don't know what the other disjunct is, we know that the claim (the disjunction as a whole) is true.

Example:

– (The Sun is a planet) & _____.

Answer:

?

Explanation:

"The Sun is a planet" is false. But, the left hand conjunct of the conjunction in question is a negation (i.e. it is a negation of the claim "The Sun is a planet."). It is saying "It is not the case that the Sun is a planet.", which is true. However, the rule for conjunction is that a conjunction is only true when both conjuncts are true. Since we don't know what the other conjunct is, we don't have enough information to determine if the claim (the conjunction as a whole) is true or false.

For the following examples, bear in mind the following information.

- MLB is a baseball league.
- The NFL is a football league.
- The NBA is a basketball league.
- The NHL is a hockey league.

1. (The NFL is a football league) & (MLB is a hockey league).

2. (The NFL is a football league) v (MLB is a hockey league).

3. – (The NHL is a basketball league).

4. – (MLB is a baseball league).

5. – – (The NBA is a basketball league).

6. (The NBA is a basketball league) → _____.

7. _____ → (The NBA is a basketball league).

8. (The NBA is a baseball league) → _____.

9. _____ → (The NBA is a baseball league).

10. (MLB is a baseball league) ↔ (The NHL is a hockey league).

11. (MLB is a football league) ↔ (The NHL is a basketball league).

12. _____ ↔ (The NHL is a hockey league).

13. – – – (The NHL is a hockey league) → – – (MLB is a hockey league).

14. _____ → (_____ v (The NFL is a football league)).

15. _____ → (_____ & (The NFL is a football league)).

Exercise 4.7

Using the 5 rules (which correspond to the 5 different operators discussed in the previous section, determine whether the following claims are true, false, or unknowable. Put "T" if the claim is true; "F" if the claim is false; and "?" if there is not enough information to determine whether or not the claim is true or false. Remember, when you see blank spaces, you aren't attempting to fill in the blank, you are attempting (when possible) to determine whether the claim as a whole is true or false – even when you don't have all of the information. Be able to explain your answer.

Example:

(Jupiter is a planet) v _____.

Answer:

T

Explanation:

"Jupiter is a planet." is true, and it is a disjunct in a disjunction. A disjunction is only false when *both* disjuncts are false, so even though we don't know what the other disjunct is, we know that the claim (the disjunction as a whole) is true.

Example:

(The Sun is a planet) & _____.

Answer:

F

Explanation:

"The Sun is a planet." is false, and it is a conjunct in a conjunction. A conjunction is only true when both conjuncts are true, so even though we don't know what the other conjunct is, we know that the claim (the conjunction as a whole) is false.

For the following examples, bear in mind the following information.

- Los Angeles is in California.
- New York City is in New York.
- Seattle is in Washington.
- St. Louis is in Missouri.

1. _____ → (Seattle is in Washington).

2. (Seattle is in California) → _____.

3. _____ v (New York City is in New York).

4. (Los Angeles is in Missouri) & _____.

5. − (Los Angeles is in Missouri) & _____.

6. (Los Angeles is in California) → (_____ & (St. Louis is in New York)).

7. (St. Louis is in Missouri) ↔ − (St. Louis is in Missouri).

8. (St. Louis is in Missouri) ↔ − (St. Louis is in California).

9. (Seattle is in New York) v (New York City is in New York).

10. _____ → (St. Louis is in California).

11. _____ → (St. Louis is in Missouri).

12. (St. Louis is in California) → _____.

13. (St. Louis is in Missouri) → _____.

14. − − − (Seattle is in Washington).

15. − − − (Seattle is in Washington) → − − (New York City is in Missouri).

Exercise 4.8

Using the 5 rules (which correspond to the 5 different operators discussed in the previous section, determine whether the following claims are true, false, or unknowable. Put "T" if the claim is true; "F" if the claim is false; and "?" if there is not enough information to determine whether or not the claim is true or false. Remember, when you see blank spaces, you aren't attempting to fill in the blank, you are attempting (when possible) to determine whether the claim as a whole is true or false – even when you don't have all of the information. Be able to explain your answer.

Example:

_____ v (Venus is a planet).

Answer:

T

Explanation:

"Venus is a planet." is true, and it is a disjunct in a disjunction. A disjunction is only false when *both* disjuncts are false, so even though we don't know what the other disjunct is, we know that the claim (the disjunction as a whole) is true.

Example:

– (The Sun is a planet) & _____.

Answer:

?

Explanation:

"The Sun is a planet" is false. But, the left hand conjunct of the conjunction in question is negated. It is saying "It is not the case that the Sun is a planet." which is true. However, the rule for conjunction is that a conjunction is only true when both conjuncts are true. Since we don't know what the other conjunct is, we don't have enough information to determine if the claim (the conjunction as a whole) is true or false.

For the following examples, bear in mind the following information.

- Chicago is in Illinois.
- Miami is in Florida.
- Dallas is in Texas.
- Phoenix is in Arizona.

1. – (Phoenix is in Arizona).

2. – (Phoenix is in Texas).

3. _____ v (Miami is in Florida).

4. _____ & (Miami is in Florida).

5. (Chicago is in Illinois) → (Chicago is in Florida).

6. (Chicago is in Florida) → (Chicago is in Illinois).

7. (Dallas is in Texas) → _____.

8. (Dallas is in Illinois) → _____.

9. (Chicago is in Illinois) → ((Miami is in Florida) v _____).

10. (Chicago is in Illinois) → ((Miami is in Florida) & _____).

11. (Chicago is in Florida) → ((Miami is in Florida) & _____).

12. (Chicago is in Florida) ↔ (Dallas is in Arizona).

13. Introduction to Logic with Dr. Heter is the finest class I have ever taken.

14. – – – (Dallas is in Texas).

15. – – – (Dallas is in Texas) → – – (Miami is in Illinois).

CHAPTER 5
Truth Tables

Chapter 5
Truth Tables

Truth Tables and Truth Conditions

Truth tables can do at least three things for us. First, they can allow us to categorize complex sentences in terms of their truth conditions. The **truth conditions** of a sentence are the conditions under which a sentence is either true or false. Second, they can help us check the validity of arguments. Third, they can help us categorize the relationship between two sentences. These latter two uses we'll come back to. For now, we are concerned with categorizing the truth conditions of sentences. A complex sentence may be either logically true, logically false, or logically contingent.

A sentence that is **logically true** is true simply because of its logical structure; it will be true no matter how the world is. Another name for a logically true sentence is a **tautology**. A sentence that is **logically false** is false simply because of its logical structure; it will be false no matter how the world is. Another name for a logically false sentence is a **self-contradiction**. A sentence that is **logically contingent** is either true or false, not simply because of its logical structure, but because of the facts in the world. Whether or not it is true or false depends upon how the world turns out to be.[90] Most (though certainly not all) sentences we utter on a day-to-day basis are logically contingent.

Now that we have those categories in place, consider the following example.

$$(P \mathbin{\&} - P) \to Q$$

Is this sentence logically true? Is it logically false? Is it logically contingent? In order to find out, we'll use a truth table.

---

90 We don't have a secondary label for a logically contingent sentences as we do for logically true sentences (i.e. "tautologies"), or logically false sentences (i.e. "self-contradictions).

The process of using a truth table has three steps.

I. Set it up.

II. Fill it in.

III. Evaluate it.

Here is our truth table after we've set it up.

P	Q	(P & - P) → Q
1. T	T	
2. T	F	
3. F	T	
4. F	F	

In the upper right hand corner we have our complex sentence that we wish to evaluate: (P & − P) → Q. In the upper left hand corner we have every simple sentence that appears in our complex sentence: P and Q. And, in the lower left hand corner we have every possible scenario represented (e.g. P and Q could both be true; P could be true, while Q could is false, P could be false, while Q is true, and P and Q could both be false). What that means is that in the lower left hand corner, we have listed every way the world could be in regard to P and Q. They could both be true; they could both be false, and so on. Now, we can fill in our truth table. We have to fill in a column for every operator in the complex sentence. So, in this sentence, we'll have three columns. We'll have one column for the conjunction (i.e. the &), one for the negation (i.e. the −), and one for the conditional (i.e. the →).

We must work from the "inside − out". That is, we must start with the operator(s) that are "operating on" the least amount of information − just the simple sentences. Then, we can move to the operators that are operating on more than just the simple sentences, until we finally fill in the column for the *main* operator, which in this case is the conditional (i.e. the →). However, we'll first start with the negation.

170

Recall that the negation means "it is not the case that". Since the negation sign is placed in front of the second P, we know that we should fill in our column so that, every time P is true, − P will be false (and therefore, should get an 'F'). Every time P is false, − P will be true (and therefore, should get a 'T'). So, our sequence should be F, F, T, T.

P	Q	(P & - P) → Q
1. T	T	F
2. T	F	F
3. F	T	T
4. F	F	T

We can now fill in the column for the conjunction (i.e. the &). Recall from our previous chapter that a conjunction is only true when both conjuncts are true. The conjuncts of this conjunction are P and − P, and in no line are both conjuncts true. In lines and 1 and 2, P is true, but − P is false. In lines 3 and 4, P is false, but − P is true. So, the sequence for this column is F, F, F, F.

P	Q	(P & - P) → Q
1. T	T	F F
2. T	F	F F
3. F	T	F T
4. F	F	F T

Finally, we can now fill in the column for the main operator, which is the conditional (i.e. the →). Recall that a conditional is only false when the antecedent is true, and the consequent is false. In this conditional, the antecedent is the conjunction, P & − P. The consequent is Q. In no line is the antecedent true when the consequent is false (because, as it turns out, in this case, in no line is the antecedent true). So, this conditional is never false; the sequence is T, T, T, T.

P	Q	(P & - P)	→ Q
1. T	T	F F	T
2. T	F	F F	T
3. F	T	F T	T
4. F	F	F T	T

We have now completed step II of our truth table – we are done filling it in! It's time to evaluate it. Recall what we said about logically true, logically false, and logically contingent sentences. A sentence that is logically true is true simply because of its logical structure; it will be true no matter how the world is. A sentence that is logically false is false simply because of its logical structure; it will be false no matter how the world is. A sentence that is logically contingent is either true or false, not simply because of its logical structure, but because of the facts in the world.

What that means for our purposes in completing our truth table is that the column for the main operator of a **logically true** sentence will be all T's. The column for the main operator for a **logically false** sentence will be all F's. And, the column for the main operator of a **logically contingent** sentence will have at least one T and at least one F.

As we can see, our truth table shows that our complex sentence, (P & – P) → Q is a tautology. By definition, a sentence is logically true (i.e. a tautology) if the column for the main operator has all T's. So, this sentences is logically true.

P	Q	(P & - P)	→ Q
1. T	T	F F	T
2. T	F	F F	T
3. F	T	F T	T
4. F	F	F T	T

The column for the main operator is all T's. So, the sentence is logically true.

172

Here is an example of a sentence that (as it turns out) is logically contingent: P ↔ (Q v R). Our truth table is set up as follows.

P Q R	P ↔ (Q v R)
1. T T T	
2. T T F	
3. T F T	
4. T F F	
5. F T T	
6. F T F	
7. F F T	
8. F F F	

We only have two operators, so we'll only need to fill in two columns. Remember, we have to work from the "inside – out". We have to start with the operators that are "operating on" the least amount of information (the simple sentences), before we can move on to the main operator. The main operator is the bi-conditional (i.e. the ↔), so that will be the final column we fill in. We'll have to start with the disjunction (i.e. the v). Remember that a disjunction will only be false when both disjuncts are false. In this case, the disjuncts are Q and R. The only lines in which both q and r are false are lines 4 and 8. So, our sequence is T, T, T, F, T, T, T, F.

P Q R	P ↔ (Q v R)
1. T T T	T
2. T T F	T
3. T F T	T
4. T F F	F
5. F T T	T
6. F T F	T
7. F F T	T
8. F F F	F

We can now fill in the column for the bi-conditional (i.e. the ↔). Remember, a bi-conditional will only be true when both components are true, or when both components are false. In this case, the components are P and the disjunction Q v R. Both components are true in lines 1, 2, and 3. Both components are false in lines 4 and 8. So, our sequence will only get T's in those lines; our sequence will be T, T, T, T, F, F, F, T.

P Q R	P ↔ (Q v R)	
1. T T T	T	T
2. T T F	T	T
3. T F T	T	T
4. T F F	T	F
5. F T T	F	T
6. F T F	F	T
7. F F T	F	T
8. F F F	T	F

Again, the bi-conditional is the main operator, so we are done filling our truth table. We are now ready to evaluate it.

P Q R	P ↔ (Q v R)	
1. T T T	T	T
2. T T F	T	T
3. T F T	T	T
4. T F F	T	F
5. F T T	F	T
6. F T F	F	T
7. F F T	F	T
8. F F F	T	F

The column for the main operator contains at least one T and at least one F. So, the sentence is logically contigent.

174

Here is just one more example already set up, filled in, and evaluated.

	P	Q	(P → Q)	↔	(P & - Q)
1.	T	T	T	F	F F
2.	T	F	F	F	T T
3.	F	T	T	F	F F
4.	F	F	T	F	F T

The column for the main operator is all F's. So, the sentence is logically false.

The column for the main operator is all F's. So, this sentence is self-contradictory. It is logically false.

The Three Laws of Thought:

It is worth pointing out that thus far, our discussion of formal logic has been based on the following three rules or "laws of thought".

1. The Law of Non-Contradiction: No proposition is both true and false. So, any sentence of the form P & – P is logically false.

2. The Law of the Excluded Middle: All propositions are either true or false. So, any sentence of the form P v – P is logically true.

3. The Law of Identity: Everything is identical with itself. So, every sentence of the form P → P is logically true.

Setting up Truth Tables Revisited

Before we proceed with exercise 5.1, it will be helpful to make sure we know how to set up a truth table. Recall that once your truth table is set up, you will need to fill in a column for every operator in you complex sentence. But, when setting up a truth table (*before* filling it), how many rows (or lines) will you need? The answer is 2^N, where N is the number of simple sentences in the complex sentence you are evaluating. So, if your complex sentence only has one simple sentence in it, you'll only have two rows. If it has two simple sentences, it will have four rows. If it has three simple sentences, it will have eight rows, and so on. Here's how your truth tables should look when you are setting them up.

If you have one simple sentence:

P	
1. T	
2. F	

If you have two simple sentences:

P	Q	
1. T	T	
2. T	F	
3. F	T	
4. F	F	

If you have three simple sentences:

P	Q	R	
1. T	T	T	
2. T	T	F	
3. T	F	T	
4. T	F	F	
5. F	T	T	
6. F	T	F	
7. F	F	T	
8. F	F	F	

If you have four simple sentences:

	P Q R S
1.	T T T T
2.	T T T F
3.	T T F T
4.	T T F F
5.	T F T T
6.	T F T F
7.	T F F T
8.	T F F F
9.	F T T T
10.	F T T F
11.	F T F T
12.	F T F F
13.	F F T T
14.	F F T F
15.	F F F T
16.	F F F F

If you have five (or more) simple sentences... then you have a real hard-nosed logic instructor, and I am sorry.

	P	Q	R	S	T	
1.	T	T	T	T	T	
2.	T	T	T	T	F	
3.	T	T	T	F	T	
4.	T	T	T	F	F	
5.	T	T	F	T	T	
6.	T	T	F	T	F	
7.	T	T	F	F	T	
8.	T	T	F	F	F	
9.	T	F	T	T	T	
10.	T	F	T	T	F	
11.	T	F	T	F	T	
12.	T	F	T	F	F	
13.	T	F	F	T	T	
14.	T	F	F	T	F	
15.	T	F	F	F	T	
16.	T	F	F	F	F	
17.	F	T	T	T	T	
18.	F	T	T	T	F	
19.	F	T	T	F	T	
20.	F	T	T	F	F	
21.	F	T	F	T	T	
22.	F	T	F	T	F	
23.	F	T	F	F	T	
24.	F	T	F	F	F	
25.	F	F	T	T	T	
26.	F	F	T	T	F	
27.	F	F	T	F	T	
28.	F	F	T	F	F	
29.	F	F	F	T	T	
30.	F	F	F	T	F	
31.	F	F	F	F	T	
32.	F	F	F	F	F	

Exercise 5.1

Construct a truth table for each of the following sentences to determine whether they are logically true, logically false, or logically contingent.

Example:

$(P \& Q) \rightarrow (P \lor Q)$

Answer:

P	Q	(P & Q)	$\rightarrow$	(P v Q)
1. T	T	T	T	T
2. T	F	F	T	T
3. F	T	F	T	T
4. F	F	F	T	F

The column for the main operator is all T's. So, the sentence is logically true.

1. $P \rightarrow (Q \lor -Q)$

2. $(P \lor Q) \leftrightarrow -(-P \rightarrow Q)$

3. $(P \rightarrow (Q \& R)) \rightarrow ((P \& Q) \rightarrow R)$

4. $P \rightarrow (Q \& -Q)$

5. $(P \& -Q) \leftrightarrow (P \rightarrow Q)$

Exercise 5.2

As in exercise 5.1, construct a truth table for each of the following sentences to determine whether they are logically true, logically false, or logically contingent.

1. $(P \lor P) \rightarrow P$

2. $(P \rightarrow Q) \rightarrow (P \leftrightarrow Q)$

3. $(P \& -P) \rightarrow Q$

4. $(P \leftrightarrow Q) \rightarrow (P \rightarrow Q)$

5. $((P \lor Q) \lor R) \rightarrow ((-P \& -Q) \rightarrow R)$

Exercise 5.3

As in Exercise 5.1, construct a truth table for each of the following sentences to determine whether they are logically true, logically false, or logically contingent.

1. $((X \rightarrow Y) \ \& \ (Y \rightarrow X)) \leftrightarrow (X \leftrightarrow Y)$ 4. $(X \ \& \ (Y \lor Z)) \leftrightarrow ((X \ \& \ Y) \lor (X \ \& \ Z))$

2. $(X \lor (Y \ \& \ Z)) \leftrightarrow ((X \lor Y) \ \& \ (X \lor Z))$ 5. $((X \rightarrow Y) \ \& \ (Y \rightarrow Z)) \rightarrow (X \rightarrow Z)$

3. $((X \lor Y) \ \& -Y) \rightarrow X$

Exercise 5.4

As in Exercise 5.1, construct a truth table for each of the following sentences to determine whether they are logically true, logically false, or logically contingent.

1. $((X \rightarrow Y) \ \& - Y) \rightarrow - X$ 4. $- (X \lor Y) \leftrightarrow (-X \ \& -Y)$

2. $(-X \rightarrow Y) \rightarrow (X \lor Y)$ 5. $(X \ \& \ X) \rightarrow X$

3. $(X \ \& -X) \rightarrow Y$

Exercise 5.5

As in Exercise 5.1, construct a truth table for each of the following sentences to determine whether they are logically true, logically false, or logically contingent.

1. $(((A \rightarrow B) \ \& \ (C \rightarrow D)) \ \& \ (A \lor C)) \rightarrow (B \lor D)$

2. $(((A \lor B) \ \& \ (C \lor D)) \ \& \ (-A \lor -C)) \rightarrow (B \lor D)$

3. $(((A \rightarrow B) \ \& \ (C \rightarrow D)) \ \& \ (- A \ \& - C)) \rightarrow (-B \ \& - D)$

4. $(((A \rightarrow B) \ \& \ (C \rightarrow D)) \ \& \ (-B \lor -D)) \rightarrow (-A \lor -C)$

5. $(-A \lor -B) \leftrightarrow (A \ \& \ B)$

Exercise 5.6

As in Exercise 5.1, construct a truth table for each of the following sentences to determine whether they are logically true, logically false, or logically contingent.

1. $((A \rightarrow B) \& A) \rightarrow B$

2. $-(((A \rightarrow B) \& -B) \rightarrow -A)$

3. $-(((A \rightarrow B) \& (B \rightarrow A)) \leftrightarrow (A \leftrightarrow B))$

4. $(A \& A) \rightarrow -A$

5. $((A \rightarrow B) \& (B \rightarrow C)) \rightarrow (A \rightarrow C)$

Truth Tables and Validity

In the previous section, we were introduced to truth tables. We also used them to categorize the truth conditions for sentences (as logically true, logically false, or logically contingent). However, as previously mentioned, truth tables can also help us check arguments for validity.

Recall that if an argument is valid, that means that it follows a proper deductive form (i.e. it really is a deductive argument). So, if an argument is valid then if the premises are true, then the conclusion must be true. Conversely, if an argument is invalid, then if the premises are true, the conclusion may still be false. What that means for us in terms of truth tables is that if an argument form is **valid**, then in every row in which the premises get a T (in the columns for their main operators), then the conclusion will get a T as well (in the column for its main operator). If an argument form is **invalid**, then there is at least one row in which all of the premises get a T (in the columns for their main operators), but the conclusion gets an F (in the column for its main operator).

Consider the following argument form.

Premise 1: $P \rightarrow (Q \vee R)$

Premise 2: – Q & – R

Therefore

Conclusion: – P

Is this a valid argument form? It's not immediately obvious, so we'll need to construct a truth table to figure it out. Here's a piece of good news. Our process for filling in a truth table will be very similar (though not completely identical) to the truth tables we've already completed. The process of using a truth table to check an argument for validity still only has three steps.

I. Set it up.

II. Fill it in.

III. Evaluate it.

Here is our truth table after we've set it up.

P Q R	Premise 1: P → (Q ∨ R)	Premise 2: - Q & - R	Conclusion: - P
1. T T T			
2. T T F			
3. T F T			
4. T F F			
5. F T T			
6. F T F			
7. F F T			
8. F F F			

Really the only difference in setting up our truth table to check for the validity of arguments (when contrasted with the truth tables in our previous section) is that we have multiple sentences to evaluate (the premises and the conclusion), so we separate them, because when we fill in our truth table, we will complete the columns for each premise and the conclusion individually. That said, in the upper right hand corner we have our sentences to evaluate (the premises, and the conclusion). In upper left hand corner we have every simple sentence that appears in those (complex) sentences (i.e. P, Q, and R). And, in the lower left hand corner, we have every possibility the way the world could be in regard to P, Q, and R. They could all be true (as in row 1). They could all be false (as in row 8). Or, they could be some combination of true and false (as in lines 2 – 7).

We are now ready start filling in our truth table. Let's start with Premise 1: P → (Q v R). Remember, we have to work from the "inside out". So, we'll have to start with the disjunction. It is a disjunction of Q and R. So, it will only be false when Q if false and R is false. The only lines in which that is the case is line 4, and 8. So, our sequence will be T, T, T F, T, T, T, F.

P Q R	Premise 1: P → (Q v R)	Premise 2: - Q & - R	Conclusion: - P
1. T T T	T		
2. T T F	T		
3. T F T	T		
4. T F F	F		
5. F T T	T		
6. F T F	T		
7. F F T	T		
8. F F F	F		

Next, we can move onto the conditional of Premise 1. The antecedent of the conditional is P. The consequent is Q v R. So, the conditional will only be false when P is true and Q v R is false. This is only the case in line 4. So our sequence will be T, T, T, F, T, T, T, T, T.

183

| | Premise 1: | | Premise 2: | Conclusion: |
P Q R	P → (Q v R)		- Q & - R	- P
1. T T T	T	T		
2. T T F	T	T		
3. T F T	T	T		
4. T F F	F	F		
5. F T T	T	T		
6. F T F	T	T		
7. F F T	T	T		
8. F F F	T	F		

Now, we can move onto Premise 2. Let's fill in – Q. Every time Q is false, – Q will be true and vice versa. So, our sequence will be F, F, T, T, F, F, T, T.

| | Premise 1: | | Premise 2: | Conclusion: |
P Q R	P → (Q v R)		- Q & - R	- P
1. T T T	T	T	F	
2. T T F	T	T	F	
3. T F T	T	T	T	
4. T F F	F	F	T	
5. F T T	T	T	F	
6. F T F	T	T	F	
7. F F T	T	T	T	
8. F F F	T	F	T	

Filling in the column for – R, every time R is true, – R will be false and vice versa. So, our sequence is F, T, F, T, F, T, F T.

| | Premise 1: | | Premise 2: | | Conclusion: |
P Q R	P → (Q v R)		- Q & - R		- P
1. T T T	T	T	F	F	
2. T T F	T	T	F	T	
3. T F T	T	T	T	F	
4. T F F	F	F	T	T	
5. F T T	T	T	F	F	
6. F T F	T	T	F	T	
7. F F T	T	T	T	F	
8. F F F	T	F	T	T	

184

Now, we may fill in the column for our conjunction. The two conjuncts are – Q and – R. Remember, the rule for conjunction is that a conjunction will only be true when both conjuncts are true. So, our sequence will be F, F, F, T, F, F, F, T.

P Q R	Premise 1: P → (Q v R)		Premise 2: - Q & - R			Conclusion: - P
1. T T T	T	T	F	F	F	
2. T T F	T	T	F	F	T	
3. T F T	T	T	T	F	F	
4. T F F	F	F	T	T	T	
5. F T T	T	T	F	F	F	
6. F T F	T	T	F	F	T	
7. F F T	T	T	T	F	F	
8. F F F	T	F	T	T	T	

Finally, we can fill in the truth conditions for our conclusion. Our conclusion is merely – P. So, it will be false every time P is true and *vice versa*. So, our sequence will be F, F, F, F, T, T, T, T.

P Q R	Premise 1: P → (Q v R)		Premise 2: - Q & - R			Conclusion: - P
1. T T T	T	T	F	F	F	F
2. T T F	T	T	F	F	T	F
3. T F T	T	T	T	F	F	F
4. T F F	F	F	T	T	T	F
5. F T T	T	T	F	F	F	T
6. F T F	T	T	F	F	T	T
7. F F T	T	T	T	F	F	T
8. F F F	T	F	T	T	T	T

Now that we have filled in our truth table, we can evaluate the information in it. However, before we do so, we should take extra precaution to make sure we do so correctly. We have filled out a total of six columns, but actually only care about the three of them. We care about the columns for the main operators. In fact, we only filled in the additional columns so that we could fill in the columns for the main operators. For instance, in regard to Premise 1, we only filled in the column for Q v R because it would allow to fill in the column for the conditional; →. In regard to Premise 2, we only filled in the columns for – Q and – R because it would allow us to fill in the column for the conjunction, &.

Before we evaluate the information in our truth table, we'll take one more precaution to make sure that we do so correctly. Remember that if an argument is valid, that means (it really is deductive and so) if the premises are true, the conclusion must be truth. In other words, the truth of the premises guarantees the truth of the conclusion. However, *validity doesn't say anything about what will be the case if (any of) the premises are false.* If an argument is valid but has false premises, the conclusion *might* be true, but it could very well be false. Because of this, in evaluating the information in our truth table, we only care about the rows in which all of the premises are true.

	Premise 1:		Premise 2:			Conclusion:
P Q R	P →	(Q v R)	– Q &	– R		– P
1. T T T	T	T	F F	F		F
2. T T F	T	T	F F	T		F
3. T F T	T	T	T F	F		F
4. T F F	F	F	T T	T		F
5. F T T	T	T	F F	F		T
6. F T F	T	T	F F	T		T
7. F F T	T	T	T F	F		T
8. F F F	T	F	T T	T		T

Take a look, in which rows are all of the premises true (I say "all of", even though we only have two premises in this argument.)? In row 1, Premise 1 is true, but Premise 2 is false (so, in evaluating the information in our truth table, row 1 is irrelevant). In row 2, it's the same situation. Premise 1 is true, but Premise 2 is false (so, row 2 is also irrelevant). When you look at each row, you'll find that the only row in which all of the premises are true is row 8 (i.e. in every other row, there is at least one false premise). So, row 8 is the only row that we care about. Because of this, *so long as you do so carefully,* you can literally cross out the other rows. When you do so, the result should be as follows.

P Q R	Premise 1: P → (Q v R)	Premise 2: - Q & - R	Conclusion: - P
1. T T T	~~T T~~	~~F F F~~	~~F~~
2. T T F	~~T T~~	~~F F T~~	~~F~~
3. T F T	~~T T~~	~~T F F~~	~~F~~
4. T F F	~~F F~~	~~T T T~~	~~F~~
5. F T T	~~T T~~	~~F F F~~	~~T~~
6. F T F	~~T T~~	~~F F T~~	~~T~~
7. F F T	~~T T~~	~~T F F~~	~~T~~
8. F F F	T F	T T T	T

There is only one row in which all of the premises are true (row 8), so (as odd as it is to say), that represents "every" row in which all of the premises are true (or, get a T). And, in that row, the conclusion is true (gets a T) as well. So, the argument is valid. Conversely, we might say that there is no row in which all of the premises are true (or, get a T), but the conclusion is false (gets an F). So, the argument is valid.

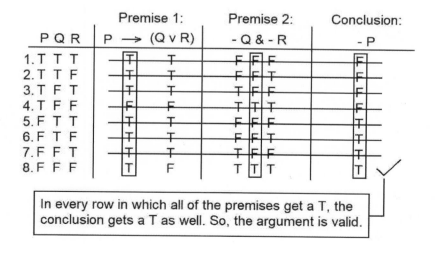

P Q R	Premise 1: P → (Q v R)	Premise 2: - Q & - R	Conclusion: - P
1. T T T	~~T T~~	~~F F F~~	~~F~~
2. T T F	~~T T~~	~~F F T~~	~~F~~
3. T F T	~~T T~~	~~T F F~~	~~F~~
4. T F F	~~F F~~	~~T T T~~	~~F~~
5. F T T	~~T T~~	~~F F F~~	~~T~~
6. F T F	~~T T~~	~~F F T~~	~~T~~
7. F F T	~~T T~~	~~T F F~~	~~T~~
8. F F F	T F	T T T	T ✓

In every row in which all of the premises get a T, the conclusion gets a T as well. So, the argument is valid.

Let's look at another example. Consider the following argument form.

Premise 1: P → Q

Premise 2: – P

Therefore,

Conclusion: – Q

Is the argument valid or invalid? We'll have to construct a truth table to check. Remember, it's a three step process: set it up, fill it in, and evaluate it. Here is our truth table set up.

P Q	Premise 1: P → Q	Premise 2: – P	Conclusion: – Q
1. T T			
2. T F			
3. F T			
4. F F			

Now that it is set up, we can fill in it. Let's start with Premise 1. Recall that a conditional is only false when the antecedent is true and the consequent is false. In regard to P → Q, that is only row 2. So, our sequence will be T, F, T T.

P Q	Premise 1: P → Q	Premise 2: – P	Conclusion: – Q
1. T T	T		
2. T F	F		
3. F T	T		
4. F F	T		

We can now fill the column for Premise 2, – P. – P (again) simply means "It is not the case that P". So, every time P is true – P will be false and vice versa. So, our sequence will be F, F, T T.

P Q	Premise 1: P → Q	Premise 2: - P	Conclusion: - Q
1. T T	T	F	
2. T F	F	F	
3. F T	T	T	
4. F F	T	T	

Finally, we can fill in the column for our Conclusion, – Q. – Q simply means "It is not the case that Q." So, every time Q is true, – Q will be false and vice versa. So, our sequence is F, T, F, T.

P Q	Premise 1: P → Q	Premise 2: - P	Conclusion: - Q
1. T T	T	F	F
2. T F	F	F	T
3. F T	T	T	F
4. F F	T	T	T

Now, we can evaluate the information in our truth table.

In this particular example, we don't have any extra columns. That is, every column that we have filled in is the main operator column for some sentence (i.e. one of the premises or the conclusion). So, we care about each column we have.

P Q	Premise 1: P → Q	Premise 2: - P	Conclusion: - Q
1. T T	T	F	F
2. T F	F	F	T
3. F T	T	T	F
4. F F	T	T	T

Recall our definition of validity. If an argument is valid then (it is really is deductive and so) if the premises are true, then the conclusion must be true. But, if the premises are false, then the conclusion could be true *or* false. So, we *only* care about the rows in which all of the premises are true. In this example, those are rows 3 and 4. So, we don't care about rows 1 and 2 (because they each contain at least one false premise).

P Q	Premise 1: P → Q	Premise 2: - P	Conclusion: - Q
1. T T	~~T~~	~~F~~	~~F~~
2. T F	~~F~~	~~F~~	~~T~~
3. F T	T	T	F
4. F F	T	T	T

As we can see, in row 4, all of the premises are true (or, get a T), and the conclusion is true (gets a T) as well. However, in row 3, The premises are true (or, get a T), but the conclusion is false (gets an F). So, the argument is invalid.

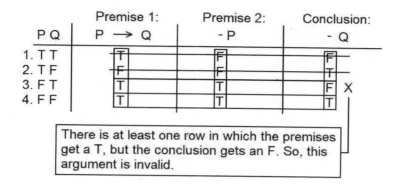

	Premise 1: P → Q	Premise 2: - P	Conclusion: - Q
P Q			
1. T T	T	F	F
2. T F	F	F	T
3. F T	T	T	F X
4. F F	T	T	T

There is at least one row in which the premises get a T, but the conclusion gets an F. So, this argument is invalid.

One thing worth addressing here is row 4. It is true that in row 4, the premises get a T and the conclusion gets a T as well. Sometimes, students are tempted to say something like "So, in row 3, the argument is invalid, but in row 4, the argument is invalid." However, this is incorrect and represents a misunderstanding of validity. The fact that in row 3 the premises get a T and the conclusion get an F means that *the entire argument form is invalid*. Remember, what it means for an argument to be valid is that (it really is deductive and so) if the premises are true, the conclusion *must* be true. In other words, it's impossible for the premises to be true and the conclusion false. So again, row 3 shows that the entire argument for in invalid. Row 4 does not change this.

Here is one additional example.

Premise 1: P → Q

Premise 2: P → R

Premise 3: – Q v – R

Therefore,

Conclusion: – P

Along with the corresponding, completed truth table.

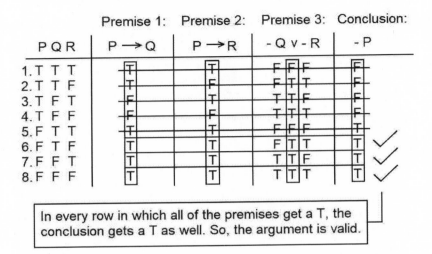

		Premise 1:	Premise 2:	Premise 3:	Conclusion:
P Q R		P → Q	P → R	- Q v - R	- P
1. T T T		T	T	F F F	F
2. T T F		T	F	F T T	F
3. T F T		F	T	T T F	F
4. T F F		F	F	T T T	F
5. F T T		T	T	F F F	T
6. F T F		T	T	F T T	T ✓
7. F F T		T	T	T T F	T ✓
8. F F F		T	T	T T T	T ✓

In every row in which all of the premises get a T, the conclusion gets a T as well. So, the argument is valid.

Filling in Truth Tables Revisited

Consider the following argument form and its corresponding truth table.

Premise 1: −P → Q

Premise 2: −Q

Therefore,

Conclusion: P

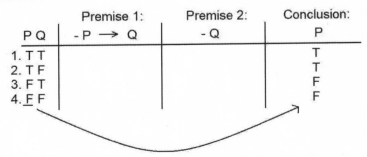

		Premise 1:	Premise 2:	Conclusion:
P Q		- P → Q	- Q	P
1. T T				T
2. T F				T
3. F T				F
4. F F				F

192

You might notice the conclusion of the argument contains no operators; it's merely a simple sentence. So, you might think that there is no column to fill in for the conclusion. While this is technically true, it will benefit you (i.e. you will be less likely to make a mistake) if you transfer over the corresponding information from the lower left hand side of the truth table as so.

And, here is the completed truth table.

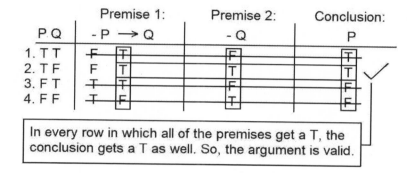

Again, while this may not be technically required, it is highly recommended. Whenever you have a premise or a conclusion that is just a simple sentence, transfer over the corresponding information from the lower left hand side of your truth table, to the lower right hand side of your truth table.

Exercise 5.7

Construct a truth table for each of the following arguments to determine whether they are valid or invalid.

Example:

Premise 1: P v Q, Premise 2: – Q, Conclusion: P

Answer:

	Premise 1:	Premise 2:	Conclusion:
P Q	P v Q	– Q	P
1. T T	T	F	T
2. T F	T	T	T
3. F T	T	F	F
4. F F	F	T	F

In every row in which all of the premises get a T, the conclusion gets a T as well. So, the argument is valid.

1. Premise 1: P → Q, Premise 2: Q → R, Conclusion: P → R

2. Premise 1: – P → – Q, Premise 2: – Q, Conclusion: – P

3. Premise 1: (P v Q) → R, Premise 2: – R, Conclusion: – P & – Q

4. Premise 1: P & Q, Premise 2: Q → R, Conclusion: – R → – P

5. Premise 1: P → Q, Premise 2: Q → P, Conclusion: P ↔ Q

Exercise 5.8

As in exercise 5.7, construct a truth table for each of the following arguments to determine whether they are valid or invalid.

1. Premise 1: A → (B v C), Premise 2: – B, Conclusion: – A

2. Premise 1: A, Conclusion: – – A

3. Premise 1: A → (B & C), Premise 2: – C, Conclusion: – A

4. Premise 1: A ↔ B, Premise 2: (A → B) → – C, Conclusion: – C

5. Premise 1: A → B, Premise 2: B v C, Premise 3: – A, Conclusion: – C

194

Exercise 5.9

As in exercise 5.7, construct a truth table for each of the following arguments to determine whether they are valid or invalid.

1. Premise 1: $(X \rightarrow Y) \rightarrow Z$, Premise 2: $- Z$, Conclusion: $X \& - Y$

2. Premise 1: $X \rightarrow Y$, Premise 2: $Y \rightarrow Z$, Conclusion: $- Z \rightarrow - X$

3. Premise 1. $X \vee Y$, Premise 2. $Y \vee Z$, Conclusion: $X \vee Z$

4. Premise 1: $X \rightarrow Y$, Premise 2: $- X$, Conclusion: $- Y$

5. Premise 1: $X \rightarrow Y$, Premise 1: $- X \rightarrow Z$, Conclusion: $Y \vee Z$

Exercise 5.10

As in exercise 5.7, construct a truth table for each of the following arguments to determine whether they are valid or invalid.

1. Premise 1: $(D \rightarrow E) \rightarrow (F \rightarrow G)$, Premise 2: $F \& - G$, Conclusion: $- (D \rightarrow E)$

2. Premise 1: $D \vee E$, Premise 2: $E \rightarrow F$, Conclusion: $- D \rightarrow F$

3. Premise 1: $D \rightarrow (E \rightarrow F)$, Premise 2: $- F \rightarrow - E$, Conclusion: $- D$

4. Premise 1: $D \leftrightarrow E$, Premise 2: $E \rightarrow F$, Premise 3: $F \vee G$, Conclusion: $G \& - D$

5. Premise 1: $D \vee (E \vee F)$, Premise 2: $- F \rightarrow - E$, Conclusion: $- D$

Exercise 5.11

In the Philosophy of Religion, one major issue is the problem of evil. The main idea is, if God exists, why does he allow (what seems to be) undue pain and suffering? Why do bad things happen (to good people or even to animals)? Below, there is one particular formation of the problem evil in argument form. Translate it into our symbolic notation. Then, construct a truth table to check whether the argument (in this form) is valid or invalid. Each sentence before the "therefore" is a premise; the sentence after the "therefore" is the conclusion.[91]

If God exists (as traditionally conceived), then God is omnipotent. If God exists (as traditionally conceived), then God is omnibenevolent. If God is omnipotent, and God is omnibenevolent, then evil does not exist. Evil does exist. <u>Therefore,</u> God does not exist (as traditionally conceived).[92]

---

91 Whether the argument is valid or invalid, the traditional theist will likely object to the third assumption. Many have done so by giving a theodicy. A theodicy is an attempt to give an account why an all-powerful, all-good God would allow evil. For a fuller exploration of this topic, see *The Problem of Evil* by Peter van Inwagen (2008).

92 Hint: this argument contains exactly 4 simple sentences.

Exercise 5.12

Rene Descartes was a 17th century French philosopher; his most famous work is the *Meditations on First Philosophy*.[93] In it, he raises a number of interesting, philosophical questions. He wants to know if he can actually *know* anything. In doing so, he comes across an argument for dualism: the idea that the mind and the body (or brain) are two separate things. It is sometimes known as "The argument from indubitability". It is reconstructed below. Translate it into our symbolic notation. Then, construct a truth table to determine whether the argument (in this form) is valid or invalid. Each sentence before the "therefore" is a premise; the sentence after the "therefore" is the conclusion.

I cannot doubt that I have a mind.[94] *I can doubt that I have a body.*[95] *If I cannot doubt that I have a mind, but I can doubt that I have a body, then it is not the case that my mind and body are identical.*[96] Therefore, *it is not the case that my mind and*[97] *body are identical.*[98]

---

93 Descartes (1993).

94 Descartes' justification for this first assumption is that he cannot doubt that he is thinking, because doubting is a form of thinking. However, a mind is a thinking thing. That is, a mind is the type of thing that doubts. So, he cannot doubt that he has a mind.

95 Descartes realizes that he believes he has a body because of his sense experience but wonders what his sense experience would be like if he were a disembodied spirit being attacked by an evil demon into falsely believing he has a body. If so, his sense experience would be exactly as it is. So, it is *possible* for him to doubt he has a body.

96 The idea here is that if two things (in this case, the mind and the brain) don't share all the same properties (i.e. one can be doubted to exist while the other cannot), then the two things are not identical. Whether or not the argument is valid, it is this premise that is perhaps the most controversial.

97 Hint: just because we have an "and" here, that doesn't necessarily mean that the argument's conclusion is a conjunction.

98 Hint: this argument contains exactly 3 simple sentences.

Exercise 5.13

In Exercise 5.12, we considered an argument for dualism from Rene Descartes. Closely related to the debate over dualism and physicalism (the idea that all that exists is the physical world) is the debate over ftee-will and determinism. (the idea that all events are predetermined from the events which preceded them, and therefore, we do not have free will).[99] Do you really have free will? Do you make genuine choices throughout your day? Or, is free-will is an illusion? Could it be that every event in your life was actually predetermined to happen the way that it did? Below is an argument that physicalism entails that human beings do not have free will. Translate it into our symbolic notation. Then, construct a truth table to determine whether the argument is valid or invalid. Each sentence before the "therefore" is a premise; the sentence after the "therefore" is the conclusion.

If physicalism is true, then every human being is nothing more than (some sort of) a biological robot. If every human being is nothing more than (some sort of) a biological robot, then every action that every human being performs is entirely dictated by the physical laws of nature. If every action that every human being performs is entirely dictated by the physical laws of nature, then no human being has free-will. <u>*Therefore*</u>*, if physicalism is true, then no human being has free-will.*[100]

---

99 For a fuller exploration of this topic, see *Free: Why Science Hasn't Disproved Free Will* by Alfred R. Mele (2014).

100 Hint: this argument contains exactly 4 simple sentences.

Exercise 5.14

The Sorites Paradox (or "a" Sorites Paradox) can be generated from any vague or "fuzzy" term. Whether or not an individual person is over 6' tall is not only easily understood, it easily determined. However, whether or not a person is "tall" is neither easily understood (at least not understood *precisely*), nor is it easily determined. Likewise, whether or not a collection of grains of sand is greater than 1 liter is easily understood and determined. However, whether or not a collection of sand counts as a "heap" of sand is neither easily understood nor determined. We could make a similar point about terms like "bald", "old", etc. This can give rise to a paradox in that from fairly uncontroversial premises, it seems as if we are able to deduce fairly implausible conclusions, (for instance) that there are no such things as heaps of sand. The argument below is an example of this. Translate it into our symbolic notation. Then, construct a truth table to determine whether the argument is valid or invalid. Each sentence before the "therefore" is a premise; the sentence after the "therefore" is the conclusion.[101]

*An individual grain of sand is not a heap of sand. No collection of grains of sand can be **turned into** a heap by adding (only) one additional grain of sand. If no collection of grains of sand can be **turned into** a heap by adding (only) one additional grain of sand, and an individual grain of sand is not a heap of sand, then there is no such thing as a heap of sand. <u>Therefore</u>, there is no such thing as a heap of sand.*[102]

---

101 For more on The Sorites Paradox, see: Hyde and Raffman (2018).
102 Hint: this argument contains exactly 3 simple sentences.

Truth Tables and Equivalence

We've now seen that truth tables are helpful for at least two things: they allow us to categorize the truth conditions for sentences, and they allow us to check the validity of arguments. However, there is one final task truth tables will allow us to master: to categorize the relationship between pairs of sentences.

Two sentences can be logically equivalent, logically contradictory, or logically contingent. Two sentences are **logically equivalent** if and only if it would be impossible for one to be true while the other is false. In other words, if two sentences are logically equivalent, the columns for their main operators will be identical. Two sentences are **logically contradictory** if and only if it would be impossible for the sentences to be simultaneously true or simultaneously false. In other words, if two sentences are logically contradictory, the columns for their main operators will be exactly the opposite from each other. Two sentences are **logically contingent** if and only if it is possible (though not necessarily the case) that they be simultaneously true or simultaneously false. In other words, if two sentences are logically contingent, the columns for their main operators will be the same in at least one row, but not every row.

Setting up and filling up a truth table to compare the truth conditions of two sentences is nearly identical to the ways in which we've already used truth tables in this chapter. Consider the following sentences.

$- (P \rightarrow Q)$

and

$P \& - Q$

And, here is a truth table set up and filled in to compare their truth conditions.

P	Q	- (P → Q)		P & - Q	
1. T	T	F	T	F	F
2. T	F	T	F	T	T
3. F	T	F	T	F	F
4. F	F	F	T	F	T

And, here is that truth table evaluated.

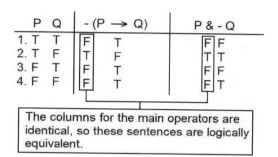

P	Q	- (P → Q)		P & - Q	
1. T	T	F	T	F	F
2. T	F	T	F	T	T
3. F	T	F	T	F	F
4. F	F	F	T	F	T

The columns for the main operators are identical, so these sentences are logically equivalent.

Because the columns for the main operators are identical, these two sentences are logically equivalent. If one is true, the other must be true, and if one is false, the other must be false as well.

Below are two additional completed (and evaluated) truth tables illustrating a pair of sentences that are logically contradictory, and a pair of sentences that are logically contingent.

P	Q	P v Q	- P & - Q		
1. T	T	T	F	F	F
2. T	F	T	F	F	T
3. F	T	T	T	F	F
4. F	F	F	T	T	T

The columns for the main operators are exactly the opposite from each other. So, these sentences are logically contradictory.

In the truth table above, because the columns for the main operators are exactly the opposite from one another, these two sentences are logically contradictory; if one is true, the other must false (and *vice versa*).

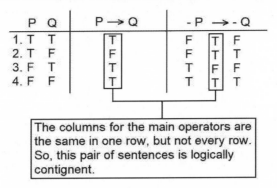

Because the columns for the main operators are the same in at least one row (in this case, rows 1 and 4) but not every row, this pair of sentences is logically contingent. They *could be* simultaneously true (or false), but whether or not that is the case depends upon the facts in the world.

Exercise 5.15

For the each of the following pairs of sentences, construct a truth table to determine whether they are logically equivalent, logically contradictory, or logically contingent.

Example:

P v – Q   (and)   – P & Q

Answer:

P Q	P v - Q	- P & Q
1. T T	T F	F F
2. T F	T T	F F
3. F T	F F	T T
4. F F	T T	T F

The columns for the main operators are exactly the opposite from each other. So, these sentences are logically contradictory.

1. P & Q	(and)	$- (P \rightarrow - Q)$
2. P $\leftrightarrow$ Q	(and)	$(P \rightarrow Q) \ \& \ (Q \rightarrow P)$
3. $- P \rightarrow Q$	(and)	$- P \ \& - Q$
4. P $\rightarrow$ Q	(and)	$- P \ v - Q$
5. $- (P \rightarrow Q)$	(and)	$- (P \ \& - Q)$

Exercise 5.16

As in exercise, 5.14, for the each of the following pairs of sentences, construct a truth table to determine whether they are logically equivalent, logically contradictory, or logically contingent.

1. X & Y	(and)	$X \rightarrow - Y$
2. $(X \ v \ Y) \leftrightarrow Z$	(and)	$- Z \leftrightarrow - (- X \ \& - Y)$
3. $X \rightarrow (Y \ \& \ Z)$	(and)	$(Y \ v \ X) \rightarrow Z$
4. $X \rightarrow Y$	(and)	$- Y \rightarrow - X$
5. $X \ v \ (Y \rightarrow Z)$	(and)	$- (- X \ \& \ (Y \ \& - Z))$

Exercise 5.17

As in exercise, 5.14, for the each of the following pairs of sentences, construct a truth table to determine whether they are logically equivalent, logically contradictory, or logically contingent.

1. $(A \rightarrow B) \leftrightarrow (C \rightarrow D)$ (and) $((A \rightarrow B) \rightarrow (C \rightarrow D))$ & $((C \rightarrow D) \rightarrow (A \rightarrow B))$

2. A (and) $- - A$

3. $A \lor (B \rightarrow C)$ (and) $- ((B \ \& - C) \ \& - A)$

4. $A \rightarrow (B \ \& \ C)$ (and) $(B \lor C) \rightarrow A$

5. $(A \lor B) \rightarrow (C \rightarrow D)$ (and) $(C \ \& - D) \rightarrow (- A \ \& - B)$

Exercise 5.18

As in exercise, 5.14, for the each of the following pairs of sentences, construct a truth table to determine whether they are logically equivalent, logically contradictory, or logically contingent.

1. $L \ \& \ (M \rightarrow N)$ (and) $- (- L \lor (M \ \& - N))$

2. $L \rightarrow L$ (and) $L \lor - L$

3. $L \leftrightarrow - M$ (and) $M \leftrightarrow - L$

4. $(L \lor M) \lor N$ (and) $L \lor (M \lor N)$

5. $(L \rightarrow M) \rightarrow N$ (and) $L \rightarrow (M \rightarrow N)$

Exercise 5.19

As in exercise, 5.14, for the each of the following pairs of sentences, construct a truth table to determine whether they are logically equivalent, logically contradictory, or logically contingent.

1. $T \rightarrow U$ (and) $- U \rightarrow - T$

2. $T \leftrightarrow (U \rightarrow V)$ (and) $T \rightarrow (U \leftrightarrow V)$

3. T v (U → V)   (and)   T v − (U & − V)

4. T & (U ↔ V)   (and)   (U → V) → − T

5. T   (and)   − − − T

CHAPTER 6
Proofs

Chapter 6

Proofs

Rules (the Good Kind)

In Chapter 5, we saw that truth tables can be extremely useful to us. They can allow us to do a number of things, including checking arguments for their validity. That said, suppose your logic instructor gave you the following argument and asked you to construct a truth table to check it for validity.

Premise 1: P → (((Q v R) & S) → (T ↔ U))

Premise 2: P

Therefore,

Conclusion: ((Q v R) & S) → (T ↔ U)

How would you feel? Upset? Would you feel upset? Would you be considering heading to the registrar's office to drop your logic class? Admittedly, that's an understandable reaction. To fill in this truth table, you would have to fill in ten columns, and (because there are six simple sentences contained in the argument) your truth table will have 64 rows!

What makes matters worse is that if you look closely, you might get the hunch that it's valid, because it looks familiar to an argument form that you've likely already seen before. Consider the following argument.

Premise 1: X → Y

Premise 2: X

Therefore,

Conclusion: Y

If you notice, in both arguments, Premise 1 is a conditional, Premise 2 is the antecedent of that conditional, and the conclusion is the consequent of that conditional. As it turns out, both these argument forms are valid.

The point is this. While our truth table method for checking the validity of arguments is perfectly well and good, it is not especially efficient. The more simple sentences you have, the size of your truth table grows exponentially. So, while our truth table system is still important to us, we will here replace it with what we might call a proof system. A proof system is a list of rules (the good kind). They aren't a list of rules about what you *can't* do. They are a list of rules about what you *can* do. Of course, the catch here is, in a proof system you can *only* do what the rules tell you that you can do.

The rules in a proof system tell you what you can infer. To put it crudely, a proof system is a set of rules that tell you "If you have *these* types of sentences, you can 'get' or infer *those* types of sentences".

At this point, the concept may only become clearer by looking at some of these rules. So, let's do just that. Our first rule is called "Modus Ponens".

1. Modus Ponens (MP): If you have a conditional, and the antecedent of that conditional, you may infer the consequent of that conditional.

Here are two examples of Modus Ponens.

$P \rightarrow Q$ $\qquad\qquad$ $(X \rightarrow Y) \rightarrow (Z \lor A)$
$\underline{Q \qquad\quad}$ $\qquad\qquad$ $\underline{X \rightarrow Y \quad}$
Q $\qquad\qquad\qquad$ $Z \lor A$

In both cases you have a conditional (on the first line), and the antecedent of that conditional (on the second line). So, you are allowed to infer the consequent of that conditional (which appears below the "inference" bar). Of course, it doesn't matter what order the sentences are listed. This too is a valid instance of Modus Ponens.

$$P$$
$$\underline{P \rightarrow Q}$$
$$Q$$

Again, the only difference in this example is the order in which the sentences are listed (but, it is the same use of the same rule: Modus Ponens).

Our second rule is called "Modus Tollens".

2. Modus Tollens (MT): If you have a conditional, and the negation of the consequent of that conditional, you may infer the negation of the antecedent of that conditional.

Here are two examples of Modus Tollens.

$$P \rightarrow Q \qquad\qquad (A \& B) \rightarrow (Z \rightarrow Q)$$
$$\underline{- Q} \qquad\qquad\qquad \underline{- (Z \rightarrow Q)}$$
$$- P \qquad\qquad\qquad - (A \& B)$$

In both cases, you have a conditional (on the first line), and the negation of the consequent of that conditional (on the second line). So, you are allowed to infer the negation of the antecedent of that conditional (which appears below the "inference" bar). As with our examples of Modus Ponens, the same holds true that it doesn't matter which order the sentences are listed. This too is a valid instance of Modus Tollens.

211

$- Q$

$\underline{P \rightarrow Q}$

$- P$

Our third rule is called "Simplification". It is fairly straightforward.

3. Simplification (Simp): If you have a conjunction, you may infer either conjunct.

Here are two examples of Simplification.

$\underline{P \& Q}$ $\underline{(X \rightarrow Y) \& (A \vee B)}$

P $A \vee B$

Q $X \rightarrow Y$

Notice, it does not matter in which order you infer the conjuncts (i.e. you may infer the left hand conjunct first, or the right hand conjunct first). Of course, the rule of Simplification states "you may infer either conjunct". It does not state that you must infer both. Here are two additional instances of Simplification which highlight this point.

$\underline{P \& Q}$ $\underline{(P \vee Q) \& (A \rightarrow B)}$

P $A \rightarrow B$

Finally (for now, anyway), our fourth rule is simply called "Conjunction", and there is a fairly simple reason for this. Consider what the rule states.

4. Conjunction (Conj): If you have any two sentences, you may infer a conjunction in which they are the conjuncts.

Here are two examples of Conjunction.

P   X → Y
Q   A → B
P & Q   (A → B) & (X → Y)

Notice, the rule of conjunction states that you may infer a conjunction of any two sentences. It does not specify in which order you must put them (the sentence listed first may be the left-hand conjunct, but it doesn't have to be).

We have now covered four rules that will make up our proof system. Though we'll add more later, this is enough for us to get started constructing proofs. Here again are our four rules (so far).

---

1. **Modus Ponens (MP):** If you have a conditional, and the antecedent of that conditional, you may infer the consequent of that conditional.

2. **Modus Tollens (MT):** If you have a conditional, and the negation of the consequent of that conditional, you may infer the negation of the antecedent of that conditional.

3. **Simplification (Simp):** If you have a conjunction, you may infer either conjunct.

4. **Conjunction (Conj):** If you have any two sentences, you may infer a conjunction in which they are the conjuncts.

Now, let's take a lot at our first proof. Here is a sequence that you might be given.

$$(P \,\&\, Q) \to R,\ P,\ Q \vdash R$$

As you perhaps noticed, there is one extra symbol that we'll have to add to our notation. It's the symbol that looks almost like a tiny turnstile, the ⊢. This is what we will call our "inference bar", and here is what it means. The sentences to the left of your inference bar are the premises. The sentence to the right of the inference bar is what you should be able to prove (given your assumptions and the rules of inference in our proof system). In other words, the inference bar is a challenge to you: if you are given the sentences on the left (in this case (P & Q) → R, P, as well as Q), prove that you can "get" or infer R, using the rules of inference at your disposal.

Here is that proof completed.

1. (P & Q) → R		A
2. P		A
3. Q		A
4. P & Q		Conj 2,3
5. R		MP 1,4

To the left, every line is numbered, just to the right of that, we have every step in our proof. And, all the way to the right, we have our "justification column". This is because, for every line in our proof, we must give a justification for every line that we have. Lines 1 – 3 are justified because those lines were given to us as assumptions. So, we just mark those with an "A" for "assumption". Line 4 is justified because of the rule of Conjunction using the lines 2 and 3. On line 2 we have P. On line 3 we have Q. And so, as the rule of Conjunction says, we may infer a conjunction of P and Q, which we do (again, on line 4), leaving us with P &Q. Line 5 is justified by the rule of Modus Ponens using lines 1 and 4. The rule of Modus Ponens says that if you have a conditional (as we do on line 1), and the antecedent of that conditional (as we do on line 4), we may infer the consequent of that conditional, which we ultimately do on line 5. Since "R" is the stated conclusion of the proof, our proof is complete.

Here's another example.

$$P \& -Q, R \rightarrow Q \vdash -R$$

And, here is the completed proof.

1. P & – Q		A
2. R → Q		A
3. – Q		Simp 1
4. – R		MT 2,3

Lines 1 and 2 are justified because those lines were given to us as assumptions. So, we just mark those with an "A" for "assumption". Line 3 is justified because of the rule of Simplification from line 1. Remember, the rule of Simplification says that if you have a conjunction (as we do on line 1), you may infer either conjunct (as we do on line 3). Line 4 is justified because of the rule of Modus Tollens using lines 2 and 3. The rule of Modus Tollens says that if you have a conditional (as we do on line 2), and the negation of the consequent of that conditional (as we don line 3), we may infer the negation of the antecedent of that conditional (and that's what we do on line 4). Since that's the stated conclusion of the proof, this proof is then complete.

Exercise 6.1

Each example below is a one-step proof. For each example, fill in *the justification column* for the one, additional step to the proof with one of our four rules: MP, MT, Simp, Conj, as well as the lines employed in the use of the rule.

Example: Answer:

1. (P → Q) → (R → S)   A   1. (P → Q) → (R → S)   A
2. P → Q   A   2. P → Q   A
3. R → S   _____   3. R → S   <u>MP 1,2</u>

Example: Answer:

1. (P → Q) & (R v S)   A   1. (P → Q) & (R v S)   A
2. R v S   _____   2. R v S   <u>Simp 1</u>

1.   **2.**
1. (X → Y) → Z   A   1. (X & Y) & Z   A
2. – Z   A   2. X & Y   _____
3. – (X → Y)   _____

3.   **4.**
1. X v Y   A   1. (X & Y) → (Z v A)   A
2. Z → X   A   2. X & Y   A
3. (X v Y) & (Z → X)   _____   3. Z v A   _____

5.   **6.**
1. X → (Y → Z)   A   1. (X & Y) → (Z v A)   A
2. – (Y → Z)   A   2. – (Z v A)   A
3. – X   _____   3. – (X & Y)   _____

7.

1. X → Y   A
2. Z & X   A
3. Z   _____

8.

1. X   A
2. Y & Z   A
3. X & (Y & Z)   _____

9.

1. X v Y   A
2. (X v Y) → (Z & A) A
3. Z & A   _____

10.

1. (X v Z) & Y   A
2. X → Y   A
3. X v Z   _____

Exercise 6.2

As in exercise 6.1, each example below is a one-step proof. For each example, fill in *the justification column* for the one, additional step to the proof with one of our 4 rules: MP, MT, Simp, Conj, as well as the lines employed in the use of the rule.

1.

1. P → (Q v R)   A
2. P   A
3. Q v R   _____

2.

1. P & Q   A
2. R → S   A
3. P   _____

3.

1. P & Q   A
2. (P & Q) → (S v T) A
3. S v T   _____

4.

1. – (P v Q)   A
2. R → (P v Q)   A
3. – R   _____

217

5.

1. P → (Q & S)   A
2. – (Q & S)   A
3. – P   _____

6.

1. P → Q   A
2. P   A
3. Q   _____

7.

1. P v Q   A
2. S v T   A
3. (S v T) & (P v Q) _____

8.

1. (P v Q) → (R v S)   A
2. P v Q   A
3. R v S   _____

9.

1. P → Q   A
2. – Q   A
3. – P   _____

10.

1. P & (R v S)   A
2. R v S   _____

Exercise 6.3

Each of the following proofs are complete, but their justification columns are yet to be filled in. Fill in each blank with the rule that justifies the line in which it is in with one of our four rules: MP, MT, Simp, Conj, as well as the lines employed in the use of the rule.

Example: Answer:

1. P → (Q v R)   A   1. P → (Q v R)   A
2. (Q v R) → S   A   2. (Q v R) → S   A
3. P   A   3. P   A
4. Q v R   _____   4. Q v R   MP 1,3
5. S   _____   5. S   MP 2,4

Example: Answer:

1. P & – Q   A   1. P & – Q   A
2. P → S   A   2. P → S   A
3. T → Q   A   3. T → Q   A
4. P   ____   4. P   Simp 1
5. – Q   ____   5. – Q   Simp 1
6. S   ____   6. S   MP 2,4
7. – T   ____   7. – T   MT 3,5
8. S & – T   ____   8. S & – T   Conj6,7

1.   **2.**

1. A → (B & C)   A   1. A → (B & C)   A
2. A   A   2. – A → D   A
3. B & C   ____   3. – (B & C)   A
4. B   ____   4. – A   ____
                                  5. D   ____

3.   **4.**

1. A   A   1. A → B   A
2. B   A   2. B → C   A
3. (A & B) → C   A   3. – C   A
4. A & B   ____   4. – B   ____
5. C   ____   5. – A   ____

219

5.

1. A & – B	A
2. A → C	A
3. C → D	A
4. A	_____
5. – B	_____
6. C	_____
7. D	_____
8. D & – B	_____

7.

1. – A → – B	A
2. – – B	A
3. – – A → C	A
4. – – A	_____
5. C	_____

6.

1. B → C	A
2. A	A
3. A → B	A
4. B	_____
5. C	_____

8.

1. A → – B	A
2. C → B	A
3. A	A
4. – B	_____
5. – C	_____
6. – C & – B	_____
7. (– C & – B) & A	_____

Exercise 6.4

As in exercise 6.3, each of the following proofs are complete, but their justification columns are yet to be filled in. Fill in each blank with the rule that justifies the line in which it is in with one of our four rules: MP, MT, Simp, Conj, as well as the lines employed in the use of the rule.

1.

1. X → Y	A
2. (X → Y) → Z	A
3. Z → Y	A
4. X → Y	A
5. Z	_____
6. Y	_____

2.

1. X & Y	A
2. X	_____
3. Y	_____
4. Y & X	_____

220

3.

1. 1. (X v Y) → Z   A
2. – Z   A
3. – (X v Y)   _____

4.

1. X & (X → Y)   A
2. X   _____
3. X → Y   _____
4. Y   _____

5.

1. – X & – Y   A
2. Z → X   A
3. – Y → A   A
4. – X   _____
5. – Y   _____
6. – Z   _____
7. A   _____
8 A & – Z   _____

6.

1. – X & (Y → X)   A
2. – X   _____
3. Y → X   _____
4. – Y   _____
5. – X & – Y   _____

7.

1. X → Y   A
2. X   A
3. Y   _____

A Strategy for Completing Proofs

Typically, when you are given a proof to solve, it will come in the form of (something like) the following sequence.

$$P → (Q \text{ \& } R), P \vdash R$$

Recall, all of the sentences to the left of the inference bar (i.e. the little turnstile shaped symbol: $\vdash$) are your assumptions. The sentence to the right of the inference bar will be the last line of your proof (i.e. it is the conclusion). It is the sentence that you are attempting to prove based on the assumptions you are given (and the rules of inference at your disposal: MP, MT, Simp, & Conj).

When you are presented with a sequence such as this to prove, you should ask yourself the following 3 questions.

1. What types of sentences do I have (in my assumptions)?

2. Do I see my conclusion (or anything like it) in my assumptions?

3. Given my answers to questions 1 and 2, what rules am I likely to use to complete this proof?

Again, the sequence in question is the following.

$$P \rightarrow (Q \& R), P \vdash R$$

1. What types of sentences do we have in our assumptions? We have a conditional, $P \rightarrow (Q \& R)$ and a simple sentence, P. In regard to the conditional, the antecedent is P, the consequent is a conjunction: Q & R.

2. Do we see our conclusion (or anything like it) in our assumptions? Our conclusion is R. And, we see that R is a conjunct of a conjunction (Q & R), and that conjunction is the consequent of a conditional.

3. Given our answers to questions 1 and 2, what rules are we likely to use? Here's one thing we can say about this sequence and eventual proof. We likely won't be using the rule of "Modus Tollens" (MT). How can we know this? We can know because in order to use MT, we have to have a negation. The rule of MT states that if you have a conditional, and the negation of the consequent, you may infer the negation of the antecedent.

Let's proceed by setting up the proof.

$$\vdash R$$

1. P → (Q & R)   A
2. P   A

We have two assumptions that we lay out on lines 1 and 2, and we justify doing so by marking those lines with an "A" in the justification column. In the upper right hand corner, we've displayed where we want to end up at the end of our proof: ⊢ R. This is not required, but it might help as a reminder of what your conclusion needs to be.

Notice that we have a conditional: P → (Q & R) on line 1, and the antecedent of that conditional on line 2: P. This is a good indication that we are going to use the rule of "Modus Ponens" (MP). If we do that, we'll end up with Q & R, and we'll be closer to our stated conclusion: R. Here is that step filled in.

$$\vdash R$$

1. P → (Q & R)   A
2. P   A
3. Q & R   MP 1,2

Again, we are justified in adding line 3 because of the rule of MP and lines 1 (where we have a conditional) and 2 (where we have the antecedent of that conditional).

Now, we have a conjunction on line 3: Q & R. Along with the rule of "Simplification" (Simp), we may infer R.

$$\vdash R$$

1. P → (Q & R)   A
2. P   A
3. Q & R   MP 1,2
4. R   Simp 3

Recall, the rule of Simp says that if you have a conjunction, you may infer either conjunct. So, that's exactly what we did on line 4. Since that's where we were supposed to end up with our original sequence, our proof is complete.

Let's consider another example. Consider the following sequences.

$$X, Y, (X \, \& \, Y) \rightarrow Z \vdash Z$$

Again, we should ask ourselves those 3 questions.

1. What types of sentences do I have (in my assumptions)?
2. Do I see my conclusion (or anything like it) in my assumptions?
3. Given my answers to questions 1 and 2, what rules am I likely to use to complete this proof?

In our assumptions, we have two simple sentences and a conditional. We see that our conclusion is Z, and that (in our assumptions), Z is the consequent of a conditional. This should lead us to think that we'll probably use the rule of MP, since MP is the only rule we have in which (when used, it) gives us the consequent of a conditional. Here is our proof set up.

$$\vdash Z$$

1. X	A
2. Y	A
3. (X & Y) → Z	A

If we had X & Y (which is the consequent of the conditional on line 3), then we could use MP to get Z. Thankfully, we have what we need to get X & Y in lines 1 and 2 (along with the rule of Conj).

224

$$\vdash Z$$

1. X   A
2. Y   A
3. (X & Y) → Z   A
4. X & Y   Conj 1,2

Now, we have what we need to complete our proof with line 5.

$$\vdash Z$$

1. X   A
2. Y   A
3. (X & Y) → Z   A
4. X & Y   Conj 1,2
5. Z   MP 3,4

On line 3 we have a conditional. On line 4 we have the antecedent of that conditional. So, on line 5, we infer the consequent of that conditional. Since that's where we were supposed to end up, our proof is complete.

Here's one more example.

$$A \rightarrow B, -B, -A \rightarrow C \vdash C$$

Ask yourself those 3 questions. 1. What types of sentences do I have (in my assumptions)? 2. Do I see my conclusion (or anything like it) in my assumptions? 3. Given my answers to questions 1 and 2, what rules am I likely to use to complete this proof?

Ultimately, we are going to use the rules of MT and MP. Here is the completed proof.

$$\vdash C$$

1. A → B	A
2. − B	A
3. − A → C	A
4. − A	MT 1,2
5. C	MP 3,4

As you begin to construct your own proofs, here's a note about citation. In order to use certain rules (e.g. MT, MP), you must have certain sentences already established in your proof. In this last proof, we used MT to justify line 4. In order to use MT, you must have a conditional and the negation of the consequent of that conditional. So, (in our justification column) we must cite the lines where we found those two sentences (lines 1 and 2). We justified line 5 because of the rule of MP, which requires us to first have a conditional and the antecedent of that conditional, so (on line 5) we cite the lines where we found those two sentences (lines 3 and 4). The general rule is this, *you must cite the lines that contain the sentences that you need in order to use the rule (as the rule is stated explicitly).*

Exercise 6.5

Using the rules of MP, MT, Simp, and Conj, complete the following proofs.

Example: Answer:

⊢ R

P → Q, Q → R, P ⊢ R

1. P → Q	A
2. Q → R	A
3. P	A
4. Q	MP 1,3
5. R	MP 2,4

226

1. M → N, – N ⊢ – M & – N

2. M → – N, O → N, M ⊢ – O

3. M → N, N → O, – O ⊢ – M

4. M & N, M → O ⊢ O

5. M → N, N → O, M ⊢ O

6. – N & (M → N) ⊢ – M

Exercise 6.6

As in exercise 6.5, using the rules of MP, MT, Simp, and Conj, complete the following proofs.

1. U → (V & – W), U & (X → W) ⊢ – X

2. U & W ⊢ W & U

3. U, (U & W) → V, W ⊢ V & U

4. V → W, V ⊢ W

5. U → W, V → X, U & – X ⊢ W & – V

6. U → (V & W), U ⊢ W & U

Exercise 6.7

As in exercise 6.5, using the rules of MP, MT, Simp, and Conj, complete the following proofs.

1. A → (B & C), (C → D) & A ⊢ D

2. A & B ⊢ B

3. – A & – B, – A → C, D → B ⊢ – D & C

4. (A & B) → C, B & A ⊢ C

5. B, A, (A & B) → (C & D) ⊢ D

6. A → B, – B ⊢ – B & – A

More (of the Good Kind) of Rules

In the previous section, we began constructing proofs based on four rules: MP, MT, Simp, and Conj. Remember, these rules are not restrictive. They don't tell us what we can't do. They tell us what we can do. In other words, they tell us what we are allowed to infer.

Our (now) fifth rule is called "Disjunctive Syllogism".

5. Disjunctive Syllogism (DS): If you have a disjunction, and the negation of one of the disjuncts, you may infer the other disjunct.

Here are two examples of Disjunctive Syllogism.

$$P \lor Q$$
$$\underline{- P}$$
$$Q$$

$$(X \rightarrow Y) \lor (Z \rightarrow A)$$
$$\underline{- (Z \rightarrow A)}$$
$$X \rightarrow Y$$

In both cases you have a disjunction (on the first line), and the negation of one of the disjuncts of that disjunction (on the second line). So, you are allowed to infer the other disjunct (which appears below the "inference" bar).

Of course, it doesn't matter what order the sentences are listed. This too is a valid instance of Disjunctive Syllogism.

$$- P$$
$$\underline{P \lor Q}$$
$$Q$$

Again, the only difference in this example is the order in which the sentences are listed (but, it is the same use of the same rule: Disjunctive Syllogism).

It is important that we don't confuse Disjunctive Syllogism and Modus Tollens. This sometimes happens because they can look somewhat similar. Here are two one-step proofs. The proof on the left employs Disjunctive Syllogism. The proof on the right employs Modus Tollens.

1. $P \lor Q$	A
2. $- Q$	A
3. P	DS1,2

1. $P \rightarrow Q$	A
2. $- Q$	A
3. $- P$	MT 1,2

Remember, when you use Disjunctive Syllogism, you have a disjunction, and the negation of the disjuncts, and you infer the other disjunct. When you use Modus Tollens, you have a conditional, and the negation of the consequent, and you infer the negation of the antecedent.

Our sixth rule is the rule of "Addition".

6. Addition (Add): If you have a sentence, you may infer a disjunction with that sentence and any other sentence as the disjuncts.

Here are two examples of the rule of Addition.

$$\frac{P}{P \lor Q} \qquad \frac{X \to Y}{(X \to Y) \lor (Z \to A)}$$

In both cases you have a sentence, and you infer a disjunction with that sentence and some other sentence as the disjuncts.

To some, the rule of Addition feels like "cheating". It feels as if we are just (in some sense) "making it up". While the rule of addition may feel weird, strange, or like it is cheating, it is nevertheless a valid rule of inference. Remember the "rule" for disjunction (in regard to truth tables) we covered in Chapter 5: a disjunction is only false when both disjuncts are false. So, (for any disjunction) if one of the disjuncts is true, the whole disjunction is true. So...

If P is true, then P ∨ Q must also be true.
If P is true, then P ∨ (X → Y) must also be true.
If P is true, P ∨ (A → (B &C)) must also be true.

If P is true, then *any* disjunction in which P appears as a disjunct will also be true. This is again because a disjunction is only false when both disjuncts are false. And, this is why the rule of Addition is valid.

Our seventh rule of inference is the rule of "Hypothetical Syllogism".

7. Hypothetical Syllogism (HS): If you have two conditionals: (i) and (ii), and the consequent of (i) is the same sentence as the antecedent of (ii), you may infer a third conditional with the antecedent of (i) and the consequent of (ii).

Here are two examples of Hypothetical Syllogism.

$$P \rightarrow Q \qquad\qquad (X \rightarrow Y) \rightarrow (Z \rightarrow A)$$
$$\underline{Q \rightarrow R} \qquad\qquad \underline{(Z \rightarrow A) \rightarrow (B \rightarrow C)}$$
$$P \rightarrow R \qquad\qquad (X \rightarrow Y) \rightarrow (B \rightarrow C)$$

In both cases, you have two conditionals in which the consequent of one conditional is the same sentence as the antecedent of the other conditional. So, you are allowed to infer a third conditional with the antecedent of the first and the consequent of the second.

Of course, it doesn't matter what order the sentences are listed. This too is a valid instance of Hypothetical Syllogism.

$$Q \rightarrow R$$
$$\underline{P \rightarrow Q}$$
$$P \rightarrow R$$

Again, the only difference in this example is the order in which the sentences are listed (but, it is the same use of the same rule: Hypothetical Syllogism).

Our eighth and final rule covered in this chapter is the rule of "Double Negation". The rule of Double Negation is what is called a rule of replacement. A **rule of replacement** is a rule of inference based on logical equivalence: if two sentences are logically equivalent, you may infer one from the other (and *vice versa*). For instance, P is logically equivalent to – – P. If P is true, then – – P must also be true, and if – – P is true, then P must also be true. This is in fact a perfect example of the (replacement) rule of "Double Negation".[103]

> **8. Double Negation (DS)**: for any sentence (i), if you assume (i), you may infer – – (i), and if you assume – – (i), you may infer (i).

Here are four different valid uses of Double Negation.

$$\frac{P}{– – P} \qquad \frac{– – P}{P} \qquad \frac{X \rightarrow Y}{– – (X \rightarrow Y)} \qquad \frac{– – (X \rightarrow Y)}{X \rightarrow Y}$$

In each example, the sentence inferred is logically equivalent to its starting assumption. And, in each case, we are only (to put it crudely) "adding" or "subtracting" two negations.

We now have four additional rules that we can add to our proof system.

---

5. **Disjunctive Syllogism (DS):** If you have a disjunction, and the negation of one of the disjuncts, you may infer the other disjunct.

6. **Addition (Add):** If you have a sentence, you may infer a disjunction with that sentence and any other sentence as the disjuncts.

7. **Hypothetical Syllogism (HS):** If you have 2 conditionals: (i) and (ii), and the consequent of (i) is the same sentence as the antecedent of (ii), you may infer a third conditional with the antecedent of (i) and the consequent of (ii).

8. **Double Negation (DN):** for any sentence (i), if you assume (i), you may infer – – (i), and if you assume – – (i), you may infer (i).

---

103 There are of course a number of additional rules of replacement that we *could* cover in this section such as **Transposition**: if $P \rightarrow Q$, you may in fer $– Q \rightarrow – P$, and if $– Q \rightarrow – P$, you may in fer $P \rightarrow Q$.

Exercise 6.8

Each example below is a one-step proof. For each example, fill in *the justification column* for the one, additional step to the proof with one of our four new rules: DS, Add, HS, or DN, as well as the lines employed in the use of the rule.

Example:1.   Answer:

1. (P v Q) v (R → S)   A   1. (P v Q) v (R → S)   A
2. – (R → S)   A   2. – (R → S)   A
3. P v Q   _____   3. P v Q   <u>DS 1,2</u>

1.   **2.**

1. P v Q   A   1. (P v Q) → (R v S)   A
2. (P v Q) v R   _____   2. (R v S) → (T v U)   A
                                    3. (P v Q) → (T v U)   _____

3.   **4.**

1. – R   A   1. – – (P → Q)   A
2. (P → Q) v R   A   2. P → Q   _____
3. P → Q   _____

5.   **6.**

1.(P & Q) v (R v S)   A   1. (P v Q) → (T → S)   A
2. – (P & Q)   A   2. (R → U) → (P v Q)   A
3. R v S   _____   3. (R → U) → (T → S)   _____

7.   **8.**

1. P v Q   A   1. P   A
2. – – (P v Q)   _____   2. (R → (S & T)) v P   _____

232

9.

1. P → Q   A
2. (P → Q) v (R v S)   _____

10.

1. P → (Q v R)   A
2. (Q v R) → S   A
3. P → S   _____

Exercise 6.9

As in exercise 6.8, each example below is a one-step proof. For each example, fill in *the justification column* for the one, additional step to the proof with one of our new four rules: DS, Add, HS, or DN, as well as the lines employed in the use of the rule.

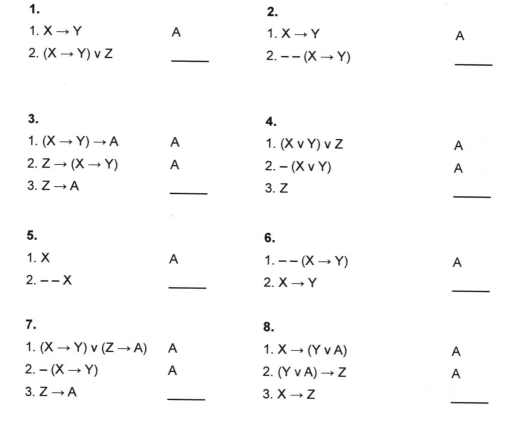

1.

1. X → Y   A
2. (X → Y) v Z   _____

2.

1. X → Y   A
2. − − (X → Y)   _____

3.

1. (X → Y) → A   A
2. Z → (X → Y)   A
3. Z → A   _____

4.

1. (X v Y) v Z   A
2. − (X v Y)   A
3. Z   _____

5.

1. X   A
2. − − X   _____

6.

1. − − (X → Y)   A
2. X → Y   _____

7.

1. (X → Y) v (Z → A)   A
2. − (X → Y)   A
3. Z → A   _____

8.

1. X → (Y v A)   A
2. (Y v A) → Z   A
3. X → Z   _____

9.

1. X	A
2. X v (Y → (Z v A))	_____

10.

1. – (X v Y)	A
2. (X v Y) v Z	A
3. Z	_____

8 Rules of Deductive Inference

1. **Modus Ponens (MP):** If you have a conditional, and the antecedent of that conditional, you may infer the consequent of that conditional.

2. **Modus Tollens (MT):** If you have a conditional, and the negation of the consequent of that conditional, you may infer the negation of the antecedent of that conditional.

3. **Simplification (Simp):** If you have a conjunction, you may infer either conjunct.

4. **Conjunction (Conj)**: If you have any two sentences, you may infer a conjunction in which they are the conjuncts.

5. **Disjunctive Syllogism (DS):** If you have a disjunction, and the negation of one of the disjuncts, you may infer the other disjunct.

6. **Addition (Add):** If you have a sentence, you may infer a disjunction with that sentence and any other sentence as the disjuncts.

7. **Hypothetical Syllogism (HS):** If you have 2 conditionals: (i) and (ii), and the consequent of (i) is the same sentence as the antecedent of (ii), you may infer a third conditional with the antecedent of (i) and the consequent of (ii).

8. **Double Negation (DN)**: for any sentence (i), if you assume (i), you may infer – – (i), and if you assume – – (i), you may infer (i).

Exercise 6.10

Using some combination of our 8 rules: MP, MT, Simp, Conj, DS, Add, HS, DN, complete the following proofs.

Example:

$X \rightarrow Y,\ X \vdash Y \vee Z$

Answer:

$\vdash Y \vee Z$

1. $X \rightarrow Y$	A	
2. X	A	
3. Y	MP 1,2	
4. Y $\vee$ Z	Add 4	

1. $P \rightarrow -Q,\ Q \vee R,\ P \vdash R$

2. $P \rightarrow Q,\ Q \rightarrow R,\ (P \rightarrow R) \rightarrow S \vdash S$

3. $P,\ (P \vee Q) \rightarrow R \vdash R$

4. $P,\ --P \rightarrow Q \vdash Q$

5. $P \rightarrow R,\ -R,\ P \vee Q \vdash Q$

6. $P,\ (P \& Q) \rightarrow -R,\ Q \vdash -R$

7. $P \rightarrow (Q \& -R),\ P,\ R \vee S \vdash S$

8. $-P \rightarrow -Q,\ Q \vdash P$

9. $P \rightarrow Q,\ P \vdash P \vee R$

10. $P \rightarrow Q,\ (Q \vee R) \rightarrow S,\ P \vdash S$

Exercise 6.11

As in exercise 6.10, using some combination of our 8 rules: MP, MT, Simp, Conj, DS, Add, HS, DN, complete the following proofs.

1. $A \rightarrow B,\ A \& C \vdash B \& C$

2. $(A \rightarrow C) \rightarrow D,\ B \rightarrow C,\ A \rightarrow B \vdash D$

3. $A,\ A \rightarrow -B,\ B \vee C \vdash C$

4. $A \rightarrow B,\ B \vee C,\ -B \vdash -A \& C$

5. $A \rightarrow B, -C, B \rightarrow C \vdash -A$　　　6. $B \rightarrow C, A \rightarrow B, A \vdash C$

7. $A \vdash A \lor (B \rightarrow C \& D))$　　　8. $-A \rightarrow -B, B \vdash A$

9. $(B \& C) \rightarrow A, C \& D, B \& E \vdash A$　　10. $A, --A \rightarrow --B \vdash B$

Exercise 6.12

As in exercise 6.10, using some combination of our 8 rules: MP, MT, Simp, Conj, DS, Add, HS, DN, complete the following proofs.

1. $X \rightarrow (Y \lor Z), X \& -Z \vdash Y$　　　2. $-(X \lor Y) \rightarrow Z, -Z \& -X \vdash Y$

3. $X \vdash X \lor (Y \& (Z \rightarrow A))$　　　4. $X \rightarrow (Y \& -Z), A \rightarrow Z, X \vdash -A$

5. $X, (X \lor Y) \rightarrow (Z \& A) \vdash A \& Z$　　6. $X \rightarrow Y, Y \rightarrow Z, (X \rightarrow Z) \rightarrow A \vdash A$

7. $X \& Y, (Y \lor Z) \rightarrow A \vdash A \lor (X \rightarrow Y)$　　8. $X \rightarrow -Y, Z \rightarrow Y, X \vdash -Z$

9. $(-X \lor Y) \rightarrow (X \lor Z), -X \vdash Z$　　10. $X \rightarrow Y, X \vdash --Y$

Exercise 6.13

As in exercise 6.10, using some combination of our 8 rules: MP, MT, Simp, Conj, DS, Add, HS, DN, complete the following proofs.

1. $M \rightarrow -(N \& L), L, N \vdash -M$　　　2. $(-M \rightarrow -N) \& N \vdash M$

3. $-M \rightarrow -N, -M, L \rightarrow N \vdash -L$　　4. $M \rightarrow -(N \lor L), N \vdash -M$

5. $(M \& N) \rightarrow L, (L \rightarrow O) \& N, M \vdash O$　　6. $M \rightarrow N, -N \lor L, M \vdash L$

7. M → − N, N v (M → L), M ⊢ L & M   8. M, (M v N) → L, (L v O) → P ⊢ P v Q

9. − M & − N, L → N, O v M ⊢ − L & O   10. M → N, M ⊢ N

Exercise 6.14

As in exercise 6.10, using some combination of our 8 rules: MP, MT, Simp, Conj, DS, Add, HS, DN, complete the following proofs.

1. U, (U v V) → (W & X) ⊢ X & U   2. U → V, V v W, − V ⊢ W & − U

3. − U → − (W v V), W ⊢ U & W   4. U ⊢ (W → V) v U

5. U → V, V → W, (U → W) → X ⊢ X   6. U → − (V & W), W, V ⊢ − U

7. U, − − U → V ⊢ U & V   8. (U & V) → W, (W → X) & V, U ⊢ X

9. U & V, (V v W) → X ⊢ X v (U → V)   10. (U → V) & − W, V → W ⊢ − U

Exercise 6.15

As in exercise 6.10, using some combination of our 8 rules: MP, MT, Simp, Conj, DS, Add, HS, DN, complete the following proofs.

1. (S → R) → (T → P), P → R, Q → P, (Q → R) → (S → P) ⊢ T → R

2. (P v Q) → (R → S), P & (T → R) ⊢ T → S

3. (P → Q) → (R & (R → S)), (T → Q) & P → T) ⊢ S v U

4. (P & Q) → (R v S), (Q & − S) & P ⊢ R

237

5. $P \rightarrow -(Q \rightarrow R), (S \rightarrow R) \& (Q \rightarrow S) \vdash -P$

6. $(P \& (P \rightarrow Q)) \& (R \rightarrow S) \& -S) \vdash Q \& -R$

7. $Q \rightarrow R, -(Q \rightarrow S) \rightarrow -(P \rightarrow R), P \rightarrow Q, \vdash P \rightarrow S$

8. $P \vdash P \vee ((R \rightarrow S) \& (T \vee (U \rightarrow V)))$

9. $P, (P \vee Q) \rightarrow R, (R \vee S) \rightarrow T, -T \vee U \vdash U \& P$

10. $-P \rightarrow -(Q \vee R), -S \rightarrow -(P \vee T), Q \vdash S \& P$

Exercise 6.16

Cultural Relativism is the view that what is morally right (and wrong) is relative to cultural agreement. That is, whether an action is right or wrong depends entirely on the moral rules established by an individual's culture. According to Cultural Relativism, the only reason *anything* is right (or wrong) is because a culture has *decided for them* that is right (or wrong). One argument against Cultural Relativism is sometimes called "The Problem of Moral Heroes": Not only is it the case that the people from history who we think of as "moral heroes" broke (or fought against) the moral rules established by their culture, but *it is for that very reason* that we consider them to be moral heroes. Jesus, Harriet Tubman, Abraham Lincoln, Gandhi, etc. are all considered moral heroes because they broke (or fought against) the moral rules of their culture. If Cultural Relativism is true, these people wouldn't be moral heroes – they're moral villains! This is again because if Cultural Relativism is true, all that there is to morality is what an individual's culture says is right and wrong. Below is a version of The Problem of Moral Heroes. Translate it into our symbolic notation. Then, construct a proof to demonstrate that the argument is valid. Each sentence before the "therefore" is one of your assumptions; the sentence after the "therefore" is the conclusion you should reach at the end of your proof.[104]

If Cultural Relativism is true, then it is always wrong for a person to break the moral rules established by their culture. Rosa Parks' fight against segregation was morally good. Rosa Parks' fight against segregation broke the moral rules established by her culture. If Rosa Parks' fight against segregation was morally good, and Rosa Parks' fight against segregation broke the moral rules established by her culture, then it is not always wrong for a person to break the moral-rules established by their culture. Therefore, Cultural Relativism is not true.[105]

---

104 For more on Cultural Relativism, see: Westacott (2020).
105 Hint: this argument contains exactly 4 simple sentences.

Exercise 6.17

In our study of truth tables in Chapter 5, we considered a version of "The Problem of Evil". Recall that according to the problem of evil, the existence of evil in the universe is said to be evidence for (or even proof of) the claim that God (as traditionally conceived) does not exist. One common response to the problem of evil is sometimes called "The Free-Will Defense". The idea is that evil's existence is compatible with God's existence (even, as traditionally conceived), because it is good that God created creatures (like you and me) with free will. However, the very existence of free will opens up the possibility of evil. That is, even though it brings evil into the world, the world would be worse if it did not contain creatures with free will. So, God has a morally justified reason for allowing evil. So, the existence of evil is not proof of (nor is it conclusive evidence for) the non-existence of God. Below is a version of The Free Will Defense. Translate it into our symbolic notation. Then, construct a proof to demonstrate that the argument is valid. Each sentence before the "therefore" is one of your assumptions; the sentence after the "therefore" is the conclusion you should reach at the end of your proof.[106]

If God's existence is not compatible with evil's existence, then God has no morally sufficient reason for allowing evil. The universe is objectively better when it is inhabited by creatures with free-will. Having free-will entails the ability to do evil. If the universe is objectively better when it is inhabited by creatures with free-will, and having the free-will entails the ability to do evil, then it would be objectively good for God to allow for evil. If it would be objectively good for God to allow for evil, then God has a morally sufficient reason for allowing evil. <u>*Therefore,*</u> *God's existence is compatible with evil's existence.*[107]

---

106 For more on the Free Will Defense, see: Plantinga (1989).
107 Hint: this argument contains exactly 5 simple sentences.

Exercise 6.18

What is meant by the claim "Beauty is in the eye of the beholder"? Presumably, it is (roughly) that beauty isn't a feature of objects in themselves; beauty is more like a feature of our *experience* of certain objects (i.e. the ones we find beautiful). The 20th Century philosopher A. J. Ayer went a step further. He endorsed what we might call "Aesthetic Non-cognitivism" according to which aesthetic judgments (e.g. "That is beautiful.", "That is ugly.", etc.) don't even express claims that are true or false. They simply express the way certain objects make us *feel*. In the passage below, he offers a brief argument based on this idea.

> "Such aesthetic words as 'beautiful' and 'hideous' are employed … not to make statements of fact, but simply to express certain feelings and evoke a certain response. It follows… that there is no sense attributing objective validity to aesthetic judgments, and no possibility of arguing about questions of value in aesthetics."[108]

Below is a reformulation of this argument. Translate it into our symbolic notation. Then, construct a proof to demonstrate that the argument is valid. Each sentence before the "therefore" is one of your assumptions; the sentence after the "therefore" is the conclusion you should reach at the end of your proof.

Aesthetic terms aren't employed to make statements of fact. Aesthetic terms are employed to express feelings. If aesthetic terms aren't employed to make statements of fact, and aesthetic terms are employed to express feelings, then there is no sense attributing objectivity to aesthetic judgments, and there is no possibility of arguing about questions of value in aesthetics. Therefore, there is no sense attributing objectivity to aesthetic judgments, and there is no possibility of arguing about questions of value in aesthetics.[109]

---

108 Ayer (1952).
109 Hint: this argument contains exactly 4 simple sentences.

Exercise 6.19

One interesting (type of) argument for the existence of God is "The Fine Tuning Argument". Just over the last generation or two, scientists have discovered that there are a number of features of the universe which, if they were just slightly different, the universe would not be a place which supports any recognizable form of complex life. Some have used this fact to craft arguments for God's existence.[110] Below is a (very broad, bare bones) reconstruction of a Fine Tuning Argument. Translate it into our symbolic notation. Then, construct a proof to demonstrate that the argument is valid. Each sentence before the "therefore" is one of your assumptions; the sentence after the "therefore" is the conclusion you should reach at the end of your proof.

Either the universe came into existence out of chance, or either the universe came into existence out of logical necessity, or the universe was purposefully created (by at least some God-like being). The universe is fine-tuned for life.[111] If the universe is fine-turned for life, then it is not the case that the universe came into existence out of chance. "Why did the universe come into existence?" is a meaningful question worthy of exploration. If "Why did the universe come into existence?" is a meaningful question worthy of exploration, then it is not the case that the universe came into existence out of logical necessity. Therefore, the universe was purposefully created (by at least some God-life being).[112]

---

110 For a fuller exploration of this topic see "Design Arguments for the Existence of God" by Kenneth Einar Himma in *The Internet Encyclopedia of Philosophy* (2018).

111 For instance "If the initial explosion of the big bang had differed in strength by as little as 1 part in 10^{60}, the universe would have either quickly collapsed back on itself or expanded too rapidly for stars to form... Calculations indicate that if the strong nuclear force... had been strong or weaker by as little as 5%, life would be impossible..." See Collins (1999), Davis (1982), Leslie (1988).

112 Hint: this argument contains exactly 5 simple sentences.

Exercise 6.20

Skepticism is the idea that knowledge has not been achieved. That is, if someone is skeptical of a claim that you have made, they don't necessarily think that what you have said was incorrect (or false). They simply think that you have not sufficiently supported your claim (with evidence) and that you don't (or perhaps, anyone else doesn't) actually *know* that what you said was true. Skepticism comes in different varieties. Global skepticism is the idea that no one knows anything. That (for most of us) seems unlikely. Local skepticism is the idea that knowledge hasn't been achieved in some particular area.[113] Below, is an argument advocating skepticism of a fairly broad sort concerning knowledge of the external world (or at least, the fact that you are an embodied person; that you are sitting here, reading this book). Translate it into our symbolic notation. Then, construct a proof to demonstrate that the argument is valid. Each sentence before the "therefore" is one of your assumptions; the sentence after the "therefore" is the conclusion you should reach at the end of your proof.

*If you cannot rule out the possibility that you are wrong about a belief B, then you do not know that B is true. If if you cannot rule out the possibility that you are wrong about a belief B, then you do not know that B is true, then if you cannot rule out the possibility that you are a brain in a vat, then you do not know that you are sitting here reading this book. If (as it turns out) you **are** a brain in a vat, then (as a brain in a vat) your experience will be identical to what it is now. If if (as it turns out) you **are** a brain in a vat, then (as a brain in a vat) your experience will be identical to what it is now, then you cannot rule out the possibility that you are a brain in a vat. Therefore, you do not know that you are sitting here reading this book..*[114]

---

113 For a fuller exploration of this topic see *The Oxford Handbook on Skepticism* by John Greco (2011).

114 Hint: this argument contains exactly 6 simple sentences.

Exercise 6.21

Is it possible to travel through (or back in) time? One issue that arises when we think about this is sometimes called "The Grandfather Paradox": if you can travel back in time, then presumably you could meet and end the life of your paternal grandfather (unintentionally or otherwise) before your father is conceived. However, if this takes place, you would never be born. And being born seems like it is a prerequisite to traveling back in time (or doing anything else, really). This, of course, is a paradox. One "solution" to the paradox is to that (perhaps) time travel is just impossible, and the only reason that we get this real result (of you leading to your own non-birth) is because we are treating it as if it *is* possible. Below is an argument to just that effect. Translate it into our symbolic notation. Then, construct a proof to demonstrate that the argument is valid. Each sentence before the "therefore" is one of your assumptions; the sentence after the "therefore" is the conclusion you should reach at the end of your proof.[115]

If it is possible for you to travel back in time, then it is possible for you to kill your (paternal) grandfather (through complete annihilation) before your father is conceived. If it is possible for you to kill your (paternal) grandfather (through complete annihilation) before your father is conceived, then it is possible for **you** *to bring about a state of affairs in which* **you** *never existed. It is not possible for* **you** *to bring about a state affairs in which* **you** *never existed. Therefore, it is not possible for you to travel back in time.*[116]

---

115 For more on philosophy and time travel, see: Smith (2019).
116 Hint: this argument contains exactly 3 simple sentences.

CHAPTER 7
Hypothetical Reasoning

Chapter 7

Hypothetical Reasoning

Consider the following case. Bill is on trial for a murder that has been well established to have occurred at 5:30 in the evening. On the night in question, Bill was spotted by numerous eye-witnesses once at 5:15 and then again at 5:45 all the way across town from where the murder took place. Bill's defense lawyer might make the following argument.

> "Suppose for the sake of argument that my client *is* guilty. That would mean that he raced across town at an unbelievable, breakneck speed during rush hour, committed the murder *without being seen*, and then raced all the way back across town at the same breakneck speed. Since no one (including and especially my client) has the capacity for that level of speed or stealth, Bill *must* be innocent; a not-guilty verdict is the only reasonable outcome of this trial."

In making this argument in this way, the defense lawyer certainly isn't committing herself to the idea that Bill is guilty, even though she opens her argument by asking us to "Suppose for the sake of argument that [Bill] *is* guilty." What she is doing is demonstrating that if we *did* assume that Bill is guilty, we would also be committing ourselves (through a bit of straightforward reasoning) to some other *unreasonable* conclusion – that Bill has a set of skills that *no one* has.

This type of hypothetical reasoning is something that we all do on a regular basis. We assume something (that we may or may not believe) for the sake of argument to see where it leads. Then, *we arrive at a conclusion that does not commit us to the truth of that original assumption*. In the example above, the defense attorney assumes that Bill is guilty for the sake of argument, shows that that assumption leads to an unreasonable conclusion (that Bill has super-speed and super-stealthiness), then infers that (because the starting assumption lead to an unreasonable conclusion) the starting assumption "for the sake of argument" that Bill is *guilty* must be false.

In this chapter, we will learn three new rules of inference, all of which employ this form of hypothetical reasoning. Together, with the first eight rules of inference we covered in Chapter 6 (MP, MT, Conj, Simp, DS, Add, HS, and DN), we will be able to prove a much larger variety of valid sequences (i.e. arguments).

Conditional Proof

Our first rule of inference to employ hypothetical reasoning is called "Conditional Proof".

> **9. Conditional Proof (CP):** If – by adding some new assumption – you can derive (i.e. infer) some new sentence, you may infer a conditional with the new assumption as the antecedent and the newly derived sentence as the consequent.

When we covered our initial eight rules, we offered a fairly straightforward visual representation of each rule (which were essentially just simple, uniform examples of each rule being used). Here was our example for Modus Ponens.

$P \rightarrow Q$

$\underline{P}$

Q

However, because Conditional Proof does not lend itself to this level of uniformity, our simple visualization will be a bit imprecise. Here it is.

P

.

.

Q

P → Q

The idea here of course is that if we assume P, and then we can derive (i.e. infer through deduction) Q, then we may infer P → Q.

Here is a sequence and a proof that employs the rule of CP.

P → Q, (P → R) → S ⊢ (Q → R) → S

1. P → Q   A
2. (P → R) → S   A
3. Q → R   A(CP)
4. P → R   HS 1,3
5. S   MP 2,4
6. (Q → R) → S   CP 3-5

In this proof, we are given two starting assumptions: P → Q, and (P → R) → S. The conclusion of the sequence is (Q → R) → S. This sequence is valid; however, if we only had our original eight rules, we could not complete this proof. With the rule of CP, we can.

Here is how the rule of CP works. It is a three step process. When you are using the rule of CP, you want to end up with a conditional. Assume the antecedent of that conditional. Then, try to "get" or "derive" the consequent of that conditional. When you do, you may infer the conditional (that you set out to end up with). That is exactly what we've done in the proof above. We want to end up with (Q → R) → S. On line 3, we assume (Q → R) for the purposes of

Conditional Proof. That's why we mark it in the justification column with "A(CP)".

Line 4 is justified by the rule of HS, using lines 1, and 3. Line 5 is justified by the rule of MP, using lines 2 and 4. What that proves then is that if Q → R is true, then S must also be true. So, we are allowed to infer (Q → R) → S because of the rule of CP; we cite the lines from when we introduced the antecedent (i.e. the new assumption) through the line we proved the consequent (i.e. the newly derived sentence): lines 3-5. You might also notice to the left of the proof is a bar that keeps track of the proof when it has an assumption "in play" that we were not initially given. On line 3, we introduce Q → R as a brand new assumption (again, this is an assumption that we were not given). So, we need to keep track of it. That assumption is still "in play" on lines 4 and 5, so we extend the bar to those lines. However, on line 6, that new assumption is "discharged". We are no longer assuming that Q → R is true. We have proven that *if* it is true, then S must be true as well. That is, we proved (Q → R) → S. So, our bar tracking the new assumption needn't extend to line 6.

Here's another example. We'll walk through it step by step. Suppose we are asked to prove the following sequence.

$$- Q \rightarrow - P \vdash P \rightarrow Q$$

The first thing that we'll need to do is to lay out the one assumption that we are given.

$$1. - Q \rightarrow - P \qquad A$$

Then, we'll want to begin the process of using the rule of CP. Remember, when you use CP, you are trying to end up with a conditional. Assume the antecedent of that conditional. We are trying to end up with P → Q; so, we assume P.

```
1. - Q →→ - P        A
  ⌐ 2. P              A(CP)
```

P is "justified" because we are adding it as an assumption for the purposes of using it in a Conditional Proof, so we label it with an "A(CP)" in the justification column. Now, we are attempting to arrive at Q (because if we do, we will have proven that P → Q). We have what it will take to get Q with the rule of MT if we just add a couple of (necessary) steps.

```
  1. - Q →→ - P       A
⌐ 2. P                A(CP)
│ 3. - - P            DN 2
```

If P is true, then (because of the rule of DN) − − P must also be true. But now, we have what we need to use MT: a conditional (on line 1) and the negation of that consequent (on line 3), so we may infer the negation of the antecedent of that conditional on line 4.

```
  1. - Q →→ - P       A
⌐ 2. P                A(CP)
│ 3. - - P            DN 2
│ 4. - - Q            MT 1,3
```

From − − Q on line 4, (because of the rule of DN again) we may infer Q on line 5.

```
  1. - Q →→ - P       A
⌐ 2. P                A(CP)
│ 3. - - P            DN 2
│ 4. - - Q            MT 1,3
└ 5. Q                DN 4
```

251

But now, we've proven what we wanted to prove. We have proven that if P is true, then Q must also be true. In other words, we have proven P → Q.

```
1. - Q → - P      A
2. P              A(CP)
3. - - P          DN 2
4. - - Q          MT 1,3
5. Q              DN 4
6. P → Q          CP 2-6
```

Remember, on line 6, we are no longer assuming that P is true, we have proven that *if* P is true, then Q must be true. In that sense, P is "discharged" as an (added) assumption. So, our bar to the left hand side does not extend down to line 6.

Here is one more step-by-step example. Suppose we are asked to prove the following sequence.

$$P \lor (Q \& R) \vdash - P \to R$$

The first thing that we'll need to do is to lay out the one assumption that we are given.

```
1. P v (Q & R)    A
```

Then, we'll want to begin the process of using the rule of CP. Remember, when you use CP, you are trying to end up with a conditional. Assume the antecedent of that conditional. We are trying to end up with – P → R; so, we assume – P.

```
1. P v (Q & R)    A
2. - P            A(CP)
```

252

According to the rule of DS, if you have a disjunction (as we do in line 1) and the negation of one of the disjuncts (as we do in line 2), you may infer the other disjunct (as we will do on line 3).

```
1. P v (Q & R)    A
2. - P            A(CP)
3. Q & R          DS 1,2
```

Using the rule of Simp, we can now infer R from Q & R (on line 4).

```
1. P v (Q & R)    A
2. - P            A(CP)
3. Q & R          DS 1,2
4. R              Simp 3
```

But now, what have we proven? We have proven that if – P is true, then R must also be true. In other words, we have proven that – P → R. Since this is the sentence we were tasked to derive (i.e. since this was the conclusion of our sequence) our proof is complete.

```
1. P v (Q & R)    A
2. - P            A(CP)
3. Q & R          DS 1,2
4. R              Simp 3
5. - P → R        CP 2-4
```

Remember, on line 5, we are no longer assuming that – P is true, we have proven that *if* – P is true, then R must be true. In that sense, – P is "discharged" as an (added) assumption. So, our bar to the left hand side does not extend down to line 5.

Exercise 7.1

Using some combination of our original 8 rules (MP, MT, Simp, Conj, DS, Add, HS, DN) and the rule of Conditional Proof (CP), complete the following proofs.

Example: $- Q \vdash (P \rightarrow Q) \rightarrow - P$

Answer:

$$
\begin{array}{lll}
1. - Q & & A \\
\left[\begin{array}{l} 2. \ P \rightarrow Q \\ 3. \ - P \end{array}\right. & & A(CP) \\
& & MT \ 1,2 \\
4. \ (P \rightarrow Q) \rightarrow -P & & CP \ 2\text{-}3
\end{array}
$$

1. $X \vdash (X \rightarrow Y) \rightarrow Y$

2. $X \rightarrow Y \vdash - Y \rightarrow - X$

3. $(X \vee Y) \rightarrow Z \vdash X \rightarrow Z$

4. $\vdash X \rightarrow (X \vee Y)$[117]

5. $\vdash (X \, \& \, (X \rightarrow Y)) \rightarrow Y$

6. $X \vee Y \vdash - X \rightarrow Y$

Exercise 7.2

As in exercise 7.1, using some combination of our original 8 rules (MP, MT, Simp, Conj, DS, Add, HS, DN) and the rule of Conditional Proof (CP), complete the following proofs.

1. $A \vdash B \rightarrow (A \, \& \, B)$

2. $- A \vdash (A \vee B) \rightarrow B$

3. $\vdash A \rightarrow - - A$

4. $A \vdash (A \rightarrow B) \rightarrow B$

5. $A \vdash (- A \vee - B) \rightarrow - B$

6. $A \rightarrow - B \vdash B \rightarrow - A$

---

117 You *can* construct a proof with no (given) assumptions. A sentence that can be proven based on no (given) assumptions is a tautology.

Exercise 7.3

As in exercise 7.1, using some combination of our original 8 rules (MP, MT, Simp, Conj, DS, Add, HS, DN) and the rule of Conditional Proof (CP), complete the following proofs.

1. ⊢ (– P & (P v Q)) → Q

2. – P → Q ⊢ – Q → P

3. P → Q ⊢ (R & P) → (R & Q)

4. ⊢ (P & Q) → (Q & P)

5. – Q ⊢ (– P → Q) → P

6. P → – Q, Q v R ⊢ P → R

Exercise 7.4

As in exercise 7.1, using some combination of our original 8 rules (MP, MT, Simp, Conj, DS, Add, HS, DN) and the rule of Conditional Proof (CP), complete the following proofs.

1. F → (G & H), I, (H & I) → J ⊢ F → J

2. (F → G) & (I → H) ⊢ (G → I) → (F → H)

3. (F v G) & (I → H), (F & – I) → J ⊢ (– H & – G) → J

4. F → G, – H → – I ⊢ (F & I) → (G & H)

5. F → G, F → H, (G & H) → I ⊢ F → I

6. ⊢ ((F & (F → G)) → G) & ((– I & (H → I)) → – H)[118]

---

118 Hint: to complete this proof, you will need to use the rule of CP two separate times.

7. (F v − G) & (G v H) ⊢ − F → H

8. ⊢ (F → G) → (− G → − F)[119]

9. ⊢ (− G → − F) → (F → G)[120]

10. F & − G ⊢ ((− F v I) & (− H → G)) → (I & H)

Exercise 7.5

As in exercise 7.1, using some combination of our original 8 rules (MP, MT, Simp, Conj, DS, Add, HS, DN) and the rule of Conditional Proof (CP), complete the following proofs.

1. U & W ⊢ ((U → V) & (W → X)) → (V & X)

2. U → (W v V) ⊢ (U & − W) → (V & U)

3. ⊢ (U & (− W → − U)) → W

4. U → − (V v W) ⊢ W → − U

5. (((U & (W → − U)) → − W) & ((X & (− X v Y)) → Y)) → Z ⊢ Z

6. U → V, W → X ⊢ (− X & − V) → (− U & − W)

7. U → V, U → W, (V & W) → X ⊢ U → X

8. − U → − (W → V) ⊢ ((W → X) & X → V)) → U

---

119 See previous footnote.
120 See previous footnote.

9. $U \rightarrow -(W \& V), W \& (X \rightarrow U) \vdash V \rightarrow -X$

10. $U \rightarrow (-W \& -V), X \rightarrow W, Y \rightarrow V \vdash U \rightarrow (-X \& -Y)$

Reductio Ad Absurdum

Our second rule of inference to employ hypothetical reasoning is called "Reductio Ad Absurdum", which means "to reduce to absurdity".

10. Reductio Ad Absurdum (RAA): If — by adding a new assumption — you can derive a contradiction, you may infer the negation of the newly added assumption.

A **contradiction** is a conjunction of any sentence and its negation. Here are some contradictions.

$P \& -P$

$(X \rightarrow Y) \& -(X \rightarrow Y)$

$(A \vee B) \& -(A \vee B)$

We know that contradictions must be false (the Law of Non-contradiction tells us this; we could construct a truth table to prove it), so anything that leads to a contradiction must also be false. If we were to give a simple (perhaps crude) visualization of the rule (as we have done with all of our previous rules), it would look like the following.

P

.

.

Q & – Q

– P

Like the rule of CP, using the rule of RAA is a three step process. When you are using the rule of RAA, you are trying to end up with or "get" a negation. Take the negation "off" and assume the remaining sentence (e.g. if you are trying to end up with – (P → Q), assume P → Q. If you are trying to end up with – X, assume X). Then, try to "get" or "derive" a contradiction: a conjunction of any sentence and its negation. If you do, you are then allowed to infer the negation of the new assumption that you added. If you assume X, and that leads to a contradiction, (since contradictions must be false), you have proven that X must be false. In other words, you have proven that – X. Here is an example of a completed proof using RAA.

$$P \& - Q \ \vdash - (P \rightarrow Q)$$

1. P & Q   A
2. P   Simp 1
3. - Q   Simp 1
4. P → Q   A(RAA)
5. Q   MP 2,4
6. Q & - Q   Conj 3,5
7. - (P → Q)   RAA 4-6

On line 1, we list out our one, given assumption. On lines 2 and 3, we use the rule of Simp to arrive at P and then – Q. On line 4, we introduce our new assumption. We are trying to "get" – (P → Q). So, if we can prove that P → Q leads to a contradiction, then we know P → Q must be false; we may infer – (P → Q). Line 5 is justified by the rule of MP using lines 2 and 4. Line 6 is merely a conjunction of 3 and 5. Line 6 is a contradiction. We know line 6 must be false (because all contradictions are false). So, whatever lead us to that contradiction (our new, added assumption: P → Q) must be false. So, on line 7, we infer the negation of that new assumption: – (P → Q). In our justification column we cite the lines from where we added the new assumption (line 4) to the line in which we derived a contradiction (line 6). To the left, we keep track of our newly added assumption until we are no longer using it. Again, we introduce it on line 4, but on line 7, we are no longer assuming that it is true. In fact we have proven that it is false. So, our bar (keeping track of our newly added assumption) shouldn't extend to line 7.

Here's one more example of a proof that will force us to use RAA. We'll walk through it step by step. Suppose we are tasked with proving the following sequence.

$$- P \, \& - Q \vdash - (P \lor Q)$$

The first thing that we'll need to do it to lay out our one, given assumption.

1. - P & - Q   A

On lines 2 and 3, we will infer both conjuncts of the conjunction – P & – Q using the rule of Simp.

1. - P & - Q   A
2. - P   Simp 1
3. - Q   Simp 1

Remember, we are attempting to prove that – (P v Q). In other words, we are attempting to prove that P v Q is false. If we can show that P v Q leads to a contradiction, we can infer – (P v Q). So, we assume P v Q in order to derive a contradiction.

```
    1. - P & - Q    A
    2. - P          Simp 1
    3. - Q          Simp 1
  ⌐ 4. P v Q        A(RAA)
```

Now, on line 5, we can infer P with the rule of DS using lines 3 and 4 to get P.

```
    1. - P & - Q    A
    2. - P          Simp 1
    3. - Q          Simp 1
  ⌐ 4. P v Q        A(RAA)
  ∟ 5. P            DS 3,4
```

Now, we have what we need to get a contradiction. We infer the conjunction of lines 2 and 5 to get P & – P.

```
    1. - P & - Q    A
    2. - P          Simp 1
    3. - Q          Simp 1
  ⌐ 4. P v Q        A(RAA)
  | 5. P            DS 3,4
  ∟ 6. P & - P      Conj 2,5
```

Since our newly added assumption, P v Q lead us to something that we know is false, P & – P we know that that new assumption must be false. So, on line 7, we infer – (P v Q).[121]

---

121 You may have noticed that we could have taken a slightly different strategy. On line 5, we use DS with lines 3 and 4 to get P, and ultimately, that leads us to the contradiction P & – P. However, we also could have used DS with lines 2 and 4 to

```
1. - P & - Q      A
2. - P            Simp 1
3. - Q            Simp 1
┌ 4. P v Q         A(RAA)
│ 5. P             DS 3,4
└ 6. P & - P       Conj 2,5
7. - (P v Q)      RAA 4-6
```

Again, to the left, we keep track of our newly added assumption until we are no longer relying on it. On line 7, we are no longer assuming that P v Q is true. We have in fact proven that it must be *false*. We have proven – (P v Q).

Exercise 7.6

Using some combination of our original 8 rules (MP, MT, Simp, Conj, DS, Add, HS, DN) and the rule of Reductio Ad Absurdum (RAA), complete the following proofs.

Example:

$P \rightarrow Q, Q \rightarrow R \vdash - (P \& - R)$

Answer:

```
1. P → Q          A
2. Q → R          A
┌ 3. P & - R       A(RAA)
│ 4. P             Simp 3
│ 5. - R           Simp 3
│ 6. Q             MP 1,4
│ 7. R             MP 2,6
└ 8. R & - R       Conj 5,7
9. - (P & - R)    RAA 3-8
```

get Q, ultimately leading us to the contradiction Q & – Q. Either strategy would be acceptable. The more complicated proofs get (especially those which require us to use rules of hypothetical reasoning), tend to be solvable with multiple (slightly varied) strategies.

1. X v Y ⊢ – (– X & – Y)　　　　　2. X & Y ⊢ – (– X v – Y)

3. X → – Y ⊢ – (X & Y)　　　　　4. X ⊢ – (X → – X)

5. X & (X → Y) ⊢ – (– X v – Y)　　6. – Y & (X → Y) ⊢ – (X v Y)

Exercise 7.7

As in Exercise 7.6, using some combination of our original 8 rules (MP, MT, Simp, Conj, DS, Add, HS, DN) and the rule of Reductio Ad Absurdum (RAA), complete the following proofs.

1. ⊢ – ((M & N) & (M → – N))[122]　　2. – M → N ⊢ – (– N & – M)

3. M → – N ⊢ – (M & N)　　　　　4. M ⊢ – (M → (N & – N))

5. ⊢ – (M & (– M v – M))　　　　　6. M v – N ⊢ – (– M & N)

Exercise 7.8

As in Exercise 7.6, using some combination of our original 8 rules (MP, MT, Simp, Conj, DS, Add, HS, DN) and the rule of Reductio Ad Absurdum (RAA), complete the following proofs.

1. – P v – Q ⊢ – (P & Q)　　　　　2. – P & – Q ⊢ – (– P → Q)

---

122 In the previous section, we learned that a sentence that can be proven based on no (given) assumptions is a tautology. This is true whether you use the rule of CP or RAA. That said, a sentence who's *negation* can be proven with no given assumptions is self-contradictory. This means that – ((M & N) & (M → – N)) is a tautology. And, (M & N) & (M → – N) is self contradictory (i.e. logically false).

3. P v Q, R → − Q ⊢ − (− P & R)   4. − P v − Q, R → Q, P → R ⊢ − P

5. P → Q, Q v P ⊢ Q[123]   6. (Q v P) & (Q v − P) ⊢ Q[124]

Exercise 7.9

As in Exercise 7.6, using some combination of our original 8 rules (MP, MT, Simp, Conj, DS, Add, HS, DN) and the rule of Reductio Ad Absurdum (RAA), complete the following proofs.

1. (A v B) & (− C → D), C → (− A & − B) ⊢ D

2. A & − B, − (A → B) → C ⊢ C

3. − (B v C), − A → B ⊢ A

4. A → B, B → (C → D), A → (C & − D) ⊢ − A

5. A → B, (A → C) & (A → − D), B → (− C v D) ⊢ − A

6. − (− C → C) → C ⊢ C

7. (A → B) → − (B v C), B ⊢ − (A → B)

---

123 Hint: this proof will require you to use the rule of DN.
124 See previous footnote.

8. $(A \rightarrow B) \rightarrow C, (-B \rightarrow -A) \rightarrow -C \vdash -(-B \rightarrow -A)$[125]

9. $(A \& B) \rightarrow C, -(A \vee D) \vee -C, B \vdash -A$

10. $B \rightarrow A, B \rightarrow -A \vdash -B$

The Principle of Explosion

The rule of RAA treats a contradiction as an "absurdity". We have (more or less) already addressed this idea. In Chapter 5, we covered the Law of Non-contradiction which states that no proposition is both true and false. Thus, all sentences of the form $P \& -P$ are logically false. However, it might benefit us to say a bit more here. One reason that we know that the Law of Non-contradiction is (or at the very least must be treated as) true is because the **Principle of Explosion** which states that if you assume a contradiction, you can prove any sentence. To put it a bit more crudely "anything follows from a contradiction". Since we know that not *every* sentence (or claim) is true, contradictions must be false.

Think of any absurd claim that you'd like. If you assume that a contradiction is true, you can prove that the absurd claim is also true. Let X stand for the following claim.

"The Loch Ness Monster's 2003 book correctly predicted that Big Foot does in fact exist."[126]

---

125 Hint: completing this proof will also force you to use the rule of CP.
126 Groening (2003).

Here is a proof of this claim (that rests only on a contradiction).

$$P \& -P \vdash X$$

1. P & -P   A
2. P   Simp 1
3. -P   Simp 1
4. P v X   Add 2
5. X   DS 3,4

The claim represented by X (that the Loch Ness Monster's 2003 book correctly predicted that Big Foot does in fact exist) was chosen at random. It could be (or could have been) any claim. But, we now have a proof that it is true based on a (randomly chosen) contradiction. If we can prove *that* claim (by assuming that a contradiction is true), we can prove *any* claim (by assuming that a contradiction is true). Again since we know that not every claim (or sentence) is true, but *everything* follows from a contradiction, contradictions are absurd (and logically false).

'Or' Elimination

Our third and final rule of hypothetical reasoning is called **'Or' Elimination**.

> **11. 'Or' Elimination (vE)**: If you have a disjunction and you can derive a new sentence by assuming both disjuncts (individually), you may infer that new sentence.

Here is our simple visualization of how the rule is intended to work.

P v Q

P

.

R

Q

.

R

R

Like CP and RAA, the use of vE has 3 steps. You are starting with a disjunction. Assume one of the disjuncts and try to get some new sentence (suppose the sentence is R). After you do so, assume the other disjunct that you started with and again get R. If you do, then the third step is just to infer the new sentence, R.

We know that if a disjunction is true, then at least one of the disjuncts is true. So, if (for instance) we assume P v Q, and by assuming P we can derive R, and then (independently of that) by assume Q we can derive R as well, then we know that R must be true. We don't know whether P is true or whether Q is true, but we know that at least one of them *has* to be true (assuming that P v Q is true). So, if both disjuncts lead to R, then R must be true. Here's a completed proof that employs the use of vE.

$$P \rightarrow R, Q \rightarrow R, P \vee Q \vdash R$$

1. $P \rightarrow R$ A
2. $Q \rightarrow R$ A
3. $P \vee Q$ A
4. P A(vE)
5. R MP 1,4
6. Q A(vE)
7. R MP 2,6
8. R vE 3,4-7

Lines 1, 2, and 3 are all given to us as assumptions. On line 4, we introduce P to show that if P is true, R must also be true (which we show on line 5 using the rule of MP). Then, on line 6 we introduce Q to show that if Q is true, R must also be true (which we show on line 7 again using the rule of MP). Again, since we know that P v Q is true, we know either P has to be true, or Q has to be true (or they are both true). Since they both "lead" to R, then R must also be true. So, we infer R on line 8. In order to use vE you need a disjunction. In the justification column, we cite the line with the disjunction (in this case, line 3), and the lines in which we introduced (and used) new assumptions.

Notice, on line 8, we are no longer assuming P and we are no longer assuming Q, we've shown that *if either* of them are true, then R must also be true. So, our bar keeping track of our added assumptions does not extend to line 8. You might also notice that our bar to the left keeping track of our added assumptions has a little added wedge right in the middle. The use of vE has two distinct parts (since you have to introduce two new assumptions). The wedge in the middle of the bar keeping track of our added assumptions marks this half way point of the use of vE.

It may be natural to ask, why do we need to again infer R on line 8? We already have it (twice!) on lines 5 and 7! While it is true that R appears on line 5 and then again on line 7, those lines are based on assumptions we were not given (P and then Q). Only the R on line 8 does not assume that P is true and it does not assume that Q is true. We know that one of them is true (because of line 3, P v Q), and we've proven through lines 4-7 that if either of them is true, R is true. So, our proof is not complete until the R on line 8.

Here's one more example of a proof that uses vE. We'll walk through it step by step. Suppose we are tasked with proving the following sequence.

$$(P \,\&\, Q) \lor (R \,\&\, Q) \;\vdash\; Q$$

The first thing that we'll of course do is lay our the one assumption that we are given.

1. (P & Q) v (R & Q)   A

We know that either P & Q is true, or R & Q is true. So, if we can "get" or derive Q from both of these sentences (individually), then Q must also be true. So, that will be our strategy: assume both disjuncts and attempt to derive Q from each of them (individually). We'll start with P & Q.

1. (P & Q) v (R & Q)   A
⌐ 2. P & Q   A(vE)

The next step is to derive or "get" Q from this added assumption.

1. (P & Q) v (R & Q)   A
⌐ 2. P & Q   A(vE)
⌊ 3. Q   Simp 2

By assuming P & Q, (for the purposes of vE), we were allowed to infer Q by using the rule of Simp from line 2. We'll be able to do the exact same thing if we assume the other half of the disjunction (on line 1), R & Q.

```
     1. (P & Q) v (R & Q)      A
  ┌  2. P & Q                  A(vE)
  │   3. Q                     Simp 2
  └  4. R & Q                  A(vE)
```

We again infer Q using the rule of Simp, this time from line 4.

```
     1. (P & Q) v (R & Q)      A
  ┌  2. P & Q                  A(vE)
  │   3. Q                     Simp 2
  │   4. R & Q                 A(vE)
  └  5. Q                      Simp 4
```

Now, what have we proven? We know that either P & Q is true, or R & Q is true. And if either of them is true, then Q is true. So, we know that Q is true. So, our proof is complete.

```
     1. (P & Q) v (R & Q)      A
  ┌  2. P & Q                  A(vE)
  │   3. Q                     Simp 2
  │   4. R & Q                 A(vE)
  └  5. Q                      Simp 4
     6. Q                      vE 1,2-5
```

Exercise 7.10

Using some combination of our original 8 rules (MP, MT, Simp, Conj, DS, Add, HS, DN) and the rule of 'Or' Elimination (vE), complete the following proofs.

Example:

P, ((P v Q) → S) v ((P v R) → S) ⊢ S

Answer:

```
1. P                               A
2. ((P v Q) → S) v ((P v R) → S)   A
3. (P v Q) → S                     A(vE)
4. P v Q                           Add 1
5. S                               MP 3,4
6. (P v R) → S                     A(vE)
7. P v R                           Add 1
8. S                               MP 6,7
9. S                               vE 2,3-8
```

1. – X v – Y, Z → X, Z → Y ⊢ – Z   2. (X → Y) & (Z → Y), X v Z ⊢ Y

3. X v Y ⊢ Y v X   4. (X v Y) v (X v Z), – X ⊢ Y v Z

5. (X v Y) v (Z → Y), – X & Z ⊢ Y   6. – X v – Z, (– Y → X) & (Z v Y) ⊢ Y

Exercise 7.11

As in exercise 7.10, using some combination of our original 8 rules (MP, MT, Simp, Conj, DS, Add, HS, DN) and the rule of 'Or' Elimination (vE), complete the following proofs.

1. A v B, – C → – A, – C → – B ⊢ C   2. A & (B v C) ⊢ (A & B) v (A & C)

3. A, ((A v B) → C) v ((A v D) → C) ⊢ C 4. (A & B) v (B & C), B → D ⊢ D

5. (A v B) & C, (A & C) → D, B → D ⊢ D 6. C → A, B → − C, − A v B ⊢ − C

Exercise 7.12

As in exercise 7.10, using some combination of our original 8 rules (MP, MT, Simp, Conj, DS, Add, HS, DN) and the rule of 'Or' Elimination (vE), complete the following proofs.

1. P v Q, − S → − (P v R), − Q v (Q → S) ⊢ S

2. (P → Q) v (− Q → R), (P & − R) & (Q → T) ⊢ T

3. (P v Q) & R, (P & R) → S, − S → − (Q & R) ⊢ S v T

4. P v Q, (P v R) → − T, (Q v S) → − T ⊢ − T & (P v Q)

5. (P → Q) & (R → Q), (S → P) v (S → R), (S → Q) → T ⊢ T & (R → Q)

6. (P & − Q) & (R → S), (− P v R) v (− R → Q) ⊢ S & P

7. (P & Q) v (R & Q) ⊢ Q

8. (P → R) v (− R → S), (P & − S) & R → T ⊢ T

271

9. $(P \& Q) \rightarrow S$, $(T \& P) \lor (R \& P)$, $Q \vdash S$

10. $(P \lor Q) \& (S \lor T)$, $(Q \lor P) \rightarrow R$, $(- T \lor U) \& (- U \rightarrow - S) \vdash R \& U$

3 Rules of Inference using Hypothetical Reasoning

9. **Conditional Proof (CP):** If – by adding some new assumption – you can derive (i.e. infer) some new sentence, you may infer a conditional with the new assumption as the antecedent, and the newly derived sentence as the consequent.

10. **Reductio Ad Absurdum (RAA):** If – by adding a new assumption – you can derive a contradiction, you may infer the negation of the newly added assumption.

11. **'Or' Elimination (vE):** If you have a disjunction and you can derive a new sentence by assuming both disjuncts (individually), you may infer that new sentence.

Exercise 7.13

Using some combination of our original 8 rules (MP, MT, Simp, Conj, DS, Add, HS, DN), as well as some combination of our 3 rules of hypothetical reasoning (CP, RAA, vE), complete the following proofs.

1. $P \rightarrow Q$, $(R \vee S) \rightarrow T$, $(Q \& T) \rightarrow U \vdash (P \& (S \vee R)) \rightarrow U$

2. $(P \rightarrow Q) \& (R \rightarrow S)$, $(Q \rightarrow T) \& (S \rightarrow T) \vdash (P \vee R) \rightarrow T$

3. $((P \rightarrow T) \& -Q) \rightarrow R$, $(Q \rightarrow S) \& (Q \rightarrow -S)$, $P \vee T \vdash R \vee U$

4. $(-P \rightarrow -Q) \rightarrow R$, $-S \rightarrow (T \rightarrow U)$, $(Q \rightarrow P) \& (T \& -U) \vdash S \& R$

5. $P \rightarrow Q$, $-Q \vdash -P$ [127]

6. $P \rightarrow Q$, $Q \rightarrow R \vdash P \rightarrow R$ [128]

7. $P \rightarrow Q$, $P \vdash Q$ [129]

---

127 In completing this particular proof, you are not allowed to use the rule of MT.
128 In completing this particular proof, you are not allowed to use the rule of HS.
129 In completing this particular proof, you are not allowed to use the rule of MP.

Exercise 7.14

Is mathematics more like a discovery, or is it more like an invention? Related to this question is the distinction between necessary and contingent truths. A truth is a contingent truth if and only if it is true but could be (or could have turned out to be) false. It is true that you are reading this book right now, but it is only contingently true (e.g. instead of choosing to read this book right now, you could have decided to watch a movie instead). In contrast, a truth is a necessary truth if and only if it is true but could not be (or could have not have turned out to be) false. Consider the claim "If you are reading this book right, then you are reading a book right now." That is not only true, it is *necessarily* true. There is no way in which that claim could turn out to be false. Below is an argument based on the idea that mathematical truths are necessary truths that leads us to conclude that mathematics is not an invention but a discovery. Translate it into our symbolic notation. Then, construct a proof to demonstrate that the argument is valid. Each sentence before the "therefore" is one of your assumptions; the sentence after the "therefore" is the conclusion you should reach at the end of your proof.

If it is not the case that mathematics is an invention, then mathematics was a discovery. If mathematics is an invention, then if "2 + 2 = 4" is true, then "2 + 2 = 4" is only contingently true. "2 + 2 = 4" is true, and "2 + 2 = 4" could not have turned out to be false. If "2 + 2 = 4" could not have turned out to be false, then "2 + 2 = 4" is necessarily true. If "2 + 2 = 4" is necessarily true, then it is not the case that "2 + 2 = 4" is only contingently true. Therefore, mathematics was a discovery.[130]

---

130 Hint: this argument contains exactly 6 simple sentences.

Exercise 7.15

Recall that physicalism is the view that all that exists is the physical world. Thus, in regard to the mind-body problem, if physicalism is true, the mind is not some extra thing that exists over and above the brain (or the body), and conscious experience is an entirely physical phenomenon. In what follows, philosopher Frank Jackson provides us with a thought experiment that will lead us to what is called "The Knowledge Argument" *against* physicalism.

"Mary is a brilliant scientist who is, for whatever reason, forced to investigate the world from a black and white room via a black and white television monitor. She specializes in neurophysiology of vision and acquires, let us suppose, all the physical information there is to obtain about what goes on when we see ripe tomatoes, or the sky, and use terms like 'red', 'blue', and so on. She discovers, for example, just which wavelength combinations from the sky stimulate the retina, and exactly how this produces via the central nervous system the contraction of the vocal cords and the expulsion of air from the lungs that results in the uttering of the sentence 'The sky is blue.'... What will happen when Mary is released from her black and white room or is given a color television monitor? Will she *learn* anything or not? It seems just obvious that she will learn something about the world and our visual experience of it. But then it is inescapable that her previous knowledge was incomplete. But she had *all* physical knowledge. Ergo there is more to have than that, and physicalism is false."[131]

Below, is a reconstruction of The Knowledge Argument. Translate it into our symbolic notation. Then, construct a proof to demonstrate that the argument is valid. Each sentence before the "therefore" is one of your assumptions; the sentence after the "therefore" is the conclusion you should reach at the end of your proof.

---

131 Jackson (1985).

275

*Mary (in the black and white room) has all of the physical information about the experience of seeing red. If physicalism is true, then if Mary (in the black and white room) has all of the physical information about the experience of seeing red, then there is nothing new Mary can learn about the experience of seeing red. Mary (in the black and white room) does not know what **it is like** to experience seeing red. If Mary (in the black and white room) does not know what **it is like** to experience seeing red, then there is something new Mary can learn about the experience of seeing red. <u>Therefore</u>, physicalism is not true.*[132]

---

132 Hint: this argument contains exactly 4 simple sentences.

Exercise 7.16

A key issue in the debate over the morality of euthanasia is whether or not there is an inherent moral difference between killing and letting die. Typically, euthanasia opponents argue that there is an inherent difference between killing and letting die, and this is an important reason to conclude that *active* euthanasia is wrong (though *passive* euthanasia is often enough morally permissible). In "A Defense of Active Euthanasia", James Rachels provides us with a thought experiment aimed at this assumption.

> "So, let us consider this pair of cases: In the first, Smith stands to gain a large inheritance if anything should happen to his six-year-old cousin. One evening while the child is taking a bath, Smith sneaks into the bathroom and drowns the child, and then arranges things so that it will look like an accident. In the second, Jones also stands to gain if anything should happen to his six-year-old cousin. Like Smith, Jones sneaks in planning to drown the child in his bath. However, just as he enters the bathroom Jones sees the child slip and hit his head, and fall face down in the water, Jones is delighted; he stands by, ready to push the child's head back under if it is necessary, but it is not necessary. With only a little thrashing about, the child drowns all by himself, 'accidentally,' as Jones watches and does nothing."[133]

Again, the purpose of the thought experiment is to provide us with an argument that there is no inherent difference between killing and letting die which is reconstructed below. Translate it into our symbolic notation. Then, construct a proof to demonstrate that the argument is valid. Each sentence before the "therefore" is one of your assumptions; the sentence after the "therefore" is the conclusion you should reach at the end of your proof.

---

133 Rachels (1975).

If there is an inherent moral difference between killing and[134] *letting die, then what Smith did was morally evil, but*[135] *what Jones did was not morally evil.*[136] *If what Smith did was morally evil, then what Jones did was morally evil.* <u>*Therefore*</u>*, There is no inherent difference between killing and letting die.*[137]

---

134 Even though there is an "and" here, it is not combing 2 simple sentences, so you do not need a conjunction in your translation of this particular sentence.

135 Don't forget, for the purposes of this exercise, "but" is interchangeable with "and".

136 Arguably, even if there is an inherent moral difference between killing and letting die, then what Jones did (i.e. merely watching his cousin drown without easily intervening) would very likely still be thought of as evil, but it would not be evil *to the same degree* or *in the same way* as what Smith did (i.e. actively drowning his cousin).

137 Hint: this argument contains exactly 3 simple sentences.

Exercise 7.17

In Chapter 5, we considered a version of "The Problem of Evil" in order to construct a truth table to check the validity of (that particular formulation of) the argument. Below is a more detailed formulation of the argument. It is worth noting that the conclusion of this version is not that God does not exist. It is that God's existence is logically incompatible with the existence of evil. Translate it into our symbolic notation. Then, construct a proof to demonstrate that the argument is valid. Each sentence before the "therefore" is one of your assumptions; the sentence after the "therefore" is the conclusion you should reach at the end of your proof.

If God exists (as traditionally conceived), then God is omnipotent. If God exists (as traditionally conceived), then God is omniscient. If God exists (as traditionally conceived), then God is omnibenevolent. If God is omnibenevolent, then God always has the desire to stop evil. If God is omnipotent, and God is omniscient, then God always has the ability to stop evil. If God always has the desire to stop evil, and God always has the ability to stop evil, then evil cannot exist. Therefore, *If God exists (as traditionally conceived), then evil cannot exist.*[138]

---

138 Hint: this argument contains exactly 7 simple sentences.

Exercise 7.18

In *Anarchy, State, and Utopia*[139], Robert Nozick defends a number of ideas central to the political philosophy of Libertarianism. The broad idea of the libertarian philosophy is that government's role in society should be extremely limited (e.g. perhaps limited to things like the a police and court systems, a national defense, infrastructure, etc.). Below is a version of a (fairly contentious) argument from Nozick that redistributive taxing is not only unjust; it amounts to *slavery*. Translate it into our symbolic notation. Then, construct a proof to demonstrate that the argument is valid. Each sentence before the "therefore" is one of your assumptions; the sentence after the "therefore" is the conclusion you should reach at the end of your proof.

If a government taxes its citizens for the purposes of wealth redistribution, then it is required of some citizens to engage in labor under threat of serious punishment to pay tax that does not benefit them. If it is required of some citizens to engage in labor under threat of serious punishment to pay tax that does not benefit them, then it is required of some citizens to engage in forced labor. Forced labor is slavery. If it is required of some citizens to engage in forced labor, and forced labor is slavery, then it is required of some citizens to be slaves. Therefore, if a government taxes its citizens for the purposes of wealth redistribution, then it is required of some citizens to be slaves.[140]

---

139 Nozick (1974).
140 Hint: this argument contains exactly 5 simple sentences.

Exercise 7.19

Scientism is (broadly speaking) the view that in order to know that something is true, it must be proven (or established) by the scientific method. One obvious problem for scientism is that scientism *itself* cannot be proven (or established) by the scientific method. It is a philosophical claim about the nature of science and knowledge. Thus, it seems as if scientism is self-refuting in that (according to its own standards) it is unknowable. Below, is an argument that spells out this problem in more detail. Translate it into our symbolic notation. Then, construct a proof to demonstrate that the argument is valid. Each sentence before the "therefore" is one of your assumptions; the sentence after the "therefore" is the conclusion you should reach at the end of your proof.[141]

The claim 'The scientific method is the only method which can establish a claim as true' cannot be established by the scientific method. If the scientific method is the only method which can establish a claim as true, then it is not the case that there is a (i.e. any) claim which can be established by a means other than the scientific method. If the scientific method is the only method which can establish a claim as true, then the claim 'The scientific method is the only method which can establish a claim as true' is true. If 'The scientific method is the only method which can establish a claim as true' is true, and the claim 'The scientific method is the only method which can establish as claim as true' cannot be established by the scientific method, then there is a (i.e. at least one) claim which can be established as true by a means other than the scientific method. Therefore, it is not the case that the scientific method is the only method which can establish a claim as true.[142]

---

141 For more on scientism (and its problems), see: Pigliucci (2018).
142 Hint: this argument contains exactly 4 simple sentences.

Exercise 7.20

Some things (e.g. The Easter Bunny, the Loch Ness Monster, etc.) don't exist. The Easter Bunny *could* exist; the Loch Ness Monster *could* exist. But, they (as far as I can tell) do not. However, there are (in contrast) things that not only do not exist, but *could not* exist. Their existence is a logical impossibility because the concept that makes up the thing itself is logically incoherent. This is true for square-circles where a *square circle is defined as a single, two dimensional object with all the features of a square and all the features of a circle*. Below is an argument – based solely on a few definitional claims – that concludes that square-circles do not (or cannot) exist. Translate it into our symbolic notation. Then, construct a proof to demonstrate that the argument is valid. Each sentence before the "therefore" is one of your assumptions; the sentence after the "therefore" is the conclusion you should reach at the end of your proof.

If a square-circle exists, then a square circle has all of the features of a square. If a square-circle exists, then a square-circle has all the features of a circle. If a square-circle has all of the features of a square, then a square-circle has corners. If a square-circle has all the features of a circle, then a square-circle's boundaries are equidistant from its center. If a square-circle's boundaries are equidistant from its center, then a square-circle does not have corners. Therefore, it is not the case that a square circle exists.[143]

---

143 Hint: this argument contains exactly 5 simple sentences.

Exercise 7.21

Naturalism is the view that all that exists is the natural world. Below is a version of an argument advanced by philosopher Alvin Plantinga called "The Evolutionary Argument Against Naturalism."[144] The idea is that (in light of what evolutionary theory tells us about ourselves) naturalism is self-defeating in the sense that if Naturalism is true, then one cannot be justified in believing that Naturalism is true. Translate the argument into symbolic notation. Then, construct a proof to demonstrate that the argument is valid. Each sentence before the "therefore" is one of your assumptions; the sentence after the "therefore" is the conclusion you should reach at the end of your proof.

If Naturalism is true, then everything about human beings is the result of natural selection. If everything about human beings is the result of natural selection, then the belief "Naturalism is true" is the result of natural selection. Natural selection is aimed at survival/reproduction as opposed to obtaining true beliefs. If the belief "Naturalism is true" is the result of natural selection, and natural selection is aimed at survival/reproduction as opposed to obtaining true beliefs, then the belief "Naturalism is true" is not justified. <u>*Therefore,*</u> *if Naturalism is true, then the belief "Naturalism is true" is not justified.*[145]

---

144 Plantinga (1993).
145 Hint: this argument contains exactly 5 simple sentences.

Works Cited

Alaimo, Kara. 2018. "Want to Purge Fake News? Try Crowdsourcing". *Bloomberg*. https://www.bloomberg.com/opinion/articles/2018-11-30/facebook-should-enlist-its-users-to-clean-up-fake-news?srnd=opinion

Aristotle. 1997. *Poetics*. Heath, Malcolm (trans.). Penguin Classics.

Aquinas, St. Thomas. 1276. Summa Theologiae. Freddoso, Alfred (trans.). www.nd.edu/~afreddos/summa-translation./TOC-part1.htm.

Ayer, A. J. 1952. *Language, Truth, and Logic*. New York: Dover.

Brisbane, Arthur. 1924. *The Book of Today*. International Magazine Company.

Baugh, Albert C. 2012. *A History of the English Language*. Routledge Books.

Bunge, Nancy. 2018. "Students Evaluating Teachers Doesn't just Hurt Teachers. It Hurts Students." *The Chronicle of Higher Education*. https://www.chronicle.com/article/Students-Evaluating-Teachers/245169

Butler, Samuel. 2016. *The Note-Books of Samuel Butler*. Jones, Henry Festing (ed.). CreateSpace Independent Publishing Platform.

Cabot, Richard C. 2010. *The Meaning of Right and Wrong*. Kessinger Publishing, LLC.

Cameron, Lisa; Dan-dan, Zhang; and Meng, Xin. 2018. "China's One-child Policy: Effects on the Sex Ratio and Crime". *Globaldev*. http://globaldev.blog/blog/china%E2%80%99s-one-child-policy-effects-sex-ratio-and-crime

Cary, Mary Kate. 2014. "Time to Lower the Drinking Age". *U.S. News and World Report*. https://www.usnews.com/opinion/articles/2014/05/07/lower-the-us-drinking-age-to-reduce-binge-drinking-and-sexual-assault

Cohen, Randy. 2000. "The Ethicist; I Want my MP3". The New York Times Magazine. https://www.nytimes.com/2000/03/26/magazine/the-way-we-live-now-3-26-00-the-ethicist-i-want-my-mp3.html

Cole, Tim. 2018. "It's Wrong for an Imperfect System to Impose an Irreversible Punishment." *Star-Telegram.* https://www.star-telegram.com/opinion/opn-columns-blogs/article219950825.html

Collins, Robin. 1999. "The Fine-Tuning Argument". *Reason for the Hope Within.* Murray, Michael J. Plantinga, Alvin (eds). Eerdmans.

Daniels, Greg. 2007. "Business School". *The Office.* Carell, Steve (performer). Deedle-Dee Productions.

Davies, Paul. 1982. *The Accidental Universe.* Cambridge University Press.

Debczak, Michele. 2017. "22 Outlawed Baby Names from Around the World." *Mental Floss.* http://mentalfloss.com/article/68768/22-outlawed-baby-names-around-world

De Los Santos, Carlos Alejandro. 2018. "The Need for Tuition Free College." *The Los Angeles Times.* https://highschool.latimes.com/garfield-senior-high-school/op-ed-the-need-for-tuition-free-college/

Descartes, Rene. 1993. *Meditations on First Philosophy.* Cress, Donald A. (trans.). Hackett Publishing Company.

Delgado, Richard. Stefancic, Jean. 2009. "Four Observations about Hate Speech". *Wake Forest Law Review.* Vol. 44.

Drayer, Lisa. 2018. "Why is Pizza so Addictive?" *CNN.* https://www.cnn.com/2018/12/06/health/pizza-addictive-food-drayer/index.html

Duhem, Pierre. 1991. *The Aim and Structure of Physical Theory.* Wiener, Philip P. (trans.). Princeton University Press.

Editorial Board, The. 2016. "Keep the Electoral College: Our View". *USA Today.* https://www.usatoday.com/story/opinion/2016/11/10/electoral-college-popular-vote-donald-trump-hillary-clinton-editorials-debates/93609562/

Editors. 2017. "Editorial: NCAA Doesn't Need to Pay Student Athletes,

Just Relax their Standards." *The Daily Free Press*. https://dailyfreepress.com/blog/2017/10/03/editorial-ncaa-doesnt-need-to-pay-student-athletes-just-relax-their-standards/

Epicurus. 1996. "Letter to Menoeceus". *Greek and Roman Philosophy after Aristotle*. Saunders, Jason (ed.). The Free Press.

Feltman, Rachel. 2016. "The Science of Fear: Why do I like Being Scared?" *The Washington Post*. https://www.washingtonpost.com/news/speaking-of-science/wp/2016/05/10/the-science-of-fear-why-do-i-like-being-scared/?noredirect=on&utm_term=.3e620f2f4e7a

Forcehimes, Andrew T. 2013. "Download this Essay: A Defence of Stealing Ebooks". *Think*. Volume 12. Issue 34. pgs. 109 – 115.

Frost, Robert. 1914. "The Death of a Hired Man". *North of Boston*. Henry Holt & Co.

Galilei, Galileo. 2001. *Dialogue Concerning the Two Chief World Systems*. Drake, Stillman (trans). Modern Library.

Gecewicz, Claire. 2018. "'New Age' Beliefs Common Among Both Religious and Nonreligious Americans". *Pew Research Center*. https://www.pewresearch.org/fact-tank/2018/10/01/new-age-beliefs-common-among-both-religious-and-nonreligious-americans/

Gilbert, Thomas. 2017. "Op-Ed: Pay Student Athletes". *The Michigan Daily*. https://www.michigandaily.com/section/viewpoints/op-ed-pay-student-athletes

Gilligan, Vince. 2016. "Switch". *Better Call Saul*. Odenkirk, Bob, Seehorn, Rhea (performers). Sony Picture Television.

Gold, Walter. 1963. "I'll Cry if I want to." *Danny*. Gore, Lesley (performer). Jones, Quincy (prod). Mercury Records.

Greco, John (ed). 2011. *The Oxford Handbook of Skepticism*. Oxford University Press.

Groening, Matt. 2003. "Spanish Fry". *Futurama*. Avanzino, Peter (dir.).

20th Century Fox Television.

Hambrick, David Z. 2018. "Your Dog May not be a Genius, After All". *Scientific American*. https://www.scientificamerican.com/article/your-dog-may-not-be-a-genius-after-all/

Heter, Joshua S. 2021. *Logic: A Guided Introduction*. The book you are reading right now.

Hood, John. 2018. "Community Colleges Deserve Better". *The News & Observer*. https://www.newsobserver.com/opinion/op-ed/article207111014.html

Himma, Kenneth Einar. 2018. "Design Arguments for the Existence of God". *The Internet Encyclopedia of Philosophy*. https://www.iep.utm.edu/design/

Huemer, Michael. 2017 "Is Taxation Theft?" https://www.libertarianism.org/columns/is-taxation-theft

Huffman, Kevin. 2015. "Standardized Testing is not Out of Control". *Pittsburgh Post-Gazette*. https://www.post-gazette.com/opinion/Op-Ed/2015/11/08/Standardized-testing-is-not-out-of-control/stories/201511080009

Hyde, Dominic and Raffman, Diana. 2018. "Sorites Paradox". *The Stanford Encyclopedia of Philosophy*. Zalta, Edward (ed.). https://plato.stanford.edu/archives/sum2018/entries/sorites-paradox/

Jackson, Frank. 1982. "Epiphenomenal Qualia". *Philosophical Quarterly*. 32. 127-35.

Johnson, Samuel. 1814. *Dictionary of the English Language*. Printed by Johnson and Warner.

Jones, Mick. Gramm, Lou. 1977. "Cold as Ice". *Foreigner*. Sinclair, John. McDonald, Ian (prods.). Atlantic Records.

Joyce, James. 2019. "Bayes' Theorem". *The Stanford Encyclopedia of Philosophy*. https://plato.stanford.edu/entries/bayes-theorem/

Kant, Immanuel. 2010. *Critique of Pure Reason*. Haywood, Francis (trans.). The British Library.

Kant, Immanuel. 1954. *The Fundamental Principles of the Metaphysics of Ethics*. Liberal Arts Press.

Kant, Immanuel. 1999. *Critique of Pure Reason*. Guyer, Paul and Wood, Allen W. (eds.) (trans). Cambridge University Press.

Kanter, Josh. Peterson, Christopher L. 2017. "Utah Families need Payday Lending Reform". *Desert News*. https://www.deseretnews.com/article/865691433/Op-ed-Utah-families-need-payday-lending-reform.html

Karjiker, Sadulla. 2013. "Justification for Copyright: The Moral Justifications". *South African Intellectual Property Law Journal*. 42.

Kim, Jaegwon. 1996. *Mind in a Physical World*. MIT Press.

Kirylo, James D. 2017. "What if we Skipped Over Testing Season?" *The State*. https://www.thestate.com/opinion/op-ed/article148797659.html

Lamont, Corliss. 1967. *Freedom of Choice Affirmed*. Horizon Press.

La Rouchefoucauld, Francois. 2020. *Maxims and Reflections*. Bund, J. W. Willis, and Friswell, J. Hain (trans.). Digireads.com.

Leibniz, Gottfried. 1991. *The Monadology*. Garber, Daniel and Ariew, Roger (trans.). Hacket Classics.

Lennon, John. 1980. "Beautiful Boy (Darling Boy)". *Double Fantasy*. Ono, Yoko (prod.). Geffen Records.

Leslie, John. 1988. "How to Draw Conclusions from a Fine-Tuned Cosmos". *Physics, Philosophy and Theology: A Common Quest for Understanding*. Vatican Observatory Press.

Lukianoff, Greg. Haidt, Jonathan. 2015. "The Coddling of the American Mind". *The Atlantic*. https://www.theatlantic.com/magazine/archive/2015/09/the-coddling-of-the-american-mind/399356/

Marcus, Gary. 2018. "A.I. is Harder than you Think". *The New York Times*. https://www.nytimes.com/2018/05/18/opinion/artificial-intelligence-challenges.html

Markie, Biz. 1989. "Just a Friend". On *The Biz Never Sleeps*. Warner

Bros. Records.

McArdle, Megan. 2017. "Living in Fear of the Internet Mob". *Chicago Tribue*. https://www.chicagotribune.com/news/opinion/commentary/ct-perspec-internet-mob-online-comments-20170823-story.html

Mele, Alfred R. 2014. *Free: Why Science Hasn't Disproved Free Will*. Oxford University Press.

Molloy, Mark. 2018. "Online Shaming: The Dangerous Rise of the Internet Pitchfork Mob". *The Telegraph*. https://www.telegraph.co.uk/news/2018/06/25/online-shaming-dangerous-rise-internet-pitchfork-mob/

Montini, E.J. 2015. "I Hate Pete Rose (who Belongs in the Hall of Fame)". https://www.azcentral.com/story/opinion/op-ed/ej-montini/2015/12/15/montini-pete-rose-hall-of-fame/77336516/

Murphy, Ryan. 2018. "Odds Against Pete Rose Being Eligible for Baseball Hall of Fame by 2020". *Sports Betting Dime*. https://www.sportsbettingdime.com/news/mlb/odds-against-pete-rose-being-eligible-for-baseball-hall-of-fame-by-2020/

Nozick, Robert. 1974. *Anarchy, State, and Utopia*. New York. Basic Books.

Osborne, Samuel. 2018. "British Couple Named Baby after Adolf Hitler, Court Hears". *Independent*. https://www.independent.co.uk/news/uk/crime/adolf-hitler-baby-national-action-trial-adam-thomas-claudia-patatas-a8576011.html

Pech, M. Scott. 2003. *The Road Less Traveled: A New Psychology of Love, Traditional Values, and Spiritual Growth*. Touchstone; Anniversary Edition.

Perez-Pena, Richard. 2012. "Studies Find More Students Cheating". *The New York Times*. https://www.nytimes.com/2012/09/08/education/studies-show-more-students-cheat-even-high-achievers.html

Pigliucci, Massimo. 2018. "The Problem with Scientism". *Blog of the APA*. https://blog.apaonline.org/2018/01/25/the-problem-with-scientism/

Plantinga, Alvin. 1989. *God, Freedom, and Evil*. Eerdmans Publishing.

Plantinga, Alvin. 1993. *Warrant and Proper Function*. Oxford University Press.

Plantinga, Alvin. 2012. "Why Darwinist Materialism is Wrong". *The New Republic*. https://newrepublic.com/article/110189/why-darwinist-materialism-wrong.

Plato. 1990. *Theaetetus*. Burnyeat, Miles (ed.). Levett, M. J. (trans.). Hackett Publishing Company.

Precht, Robert. 2006. "Japan the Jury". *The New York Times*. https://www.nytimes.com/2006/12/01/opinion/01precht.html?mtrref=www.google.com&gwh=8BA0BEBBF20D81F5E276131935EAF03C&gwt=pay&assetType=opinion

Rachels, James. 1975. "Active and Passive Euthanasia". *New England Journal of Medicine*. 292.

Risinger, Nathan. 2012. "The Ethics of Football Helmets". *Bioethics Bulletin*. http://bioethicsbulletin.org/archive/op-ed-the-ethics-of-football-helmets.

Ruston, Delaney. 2017. "Smartphones aren't a Smart Choice in Middle School". *CNN*. https://www.cnn.com/2017/12/22/opinions/smartphones-middle-school-opinion-ruston/index.html

Segal, Erich. 1971. *Love Story*. Hoffmann und Campe Verlag.

Seigel, Ethan. 2016: "Why College is so Expensive, and How to Fix it." *Forbes*. https://www.forbes.com/sites/startswithabang/2016/03/01/why-college-is-so-expensive-and-how-to-fix-it/#42738bd252f1

Seinfeld, Jerry. David, Larry. 1994. "The Marine Biologist". *Seinfeld*. . Alexander, Jason (performer). Castle Rock Entertainment.

Shakespeare, William. 1591. *Henry VI, Part II*. http://shakespeare.mit.edu/2henryvi/full.html

Shakespeare, William. 1624. *Julius Caesar*. http://shakespeare.mit.edu/julius_caesar/full.html

Silverman, Michael. 2015. "Roger Clemons, Barry Bonds get my Vote".

The Boston Herald. https://www.bostonherald.com/2015/12/26/silverman-roger-clemens-barry-bonds-get-my-vote/

Smith, Chris. 2012. "Why it's Time to Legalize Steroids in Professional Sports." *Forbes*. https://www.forbes.com/sites/chrissmith/2012/08/24/why-its-time-to-legalize-steroids-in-professional-sports/#33d8708165d2

Smith, Nicholas J. J. 2019. "Time Travel". *The Stanford Encyclopedia of Philosophy*. https://plato.stanford.edu/archives/sum2019/entries/time-travel. Zalta, Edward N. (ed).

Stump, Eleonore. 2012. *Wandering in Darkness Narrative and the Problem of Suffering*. Oxford University Press.

Teehan, John. 2006. "A Holiday Season for Atheists, Too". *The New York Times*.

Tolstoy, Leo. 2013. *What is Art?* Maude, Aylmer (trans.). DigiReads.com Publishing.

Ubinas, Luisa A. and Gabrieli, Chris. 2011. "Shortchanged by the Bell". *The New York Times*. https://www.nytimes.com/2011/08/23/opinion/shortchanged-by-the-school-bell.html

United Nations. 1985. *United Nations Convention Against Torture*. https://www.law.cornell.edu/cfr/text/22/95.1

VanDerWerff, Todd. 2018. "9 Time Mr. Rogers said Exactly the Right thing". *Vox*. https://www.vox.com/culture/2017/5/23/15681060/celebrating-mister-rogers-google-doodle-anniversary-quotes

Van Inwagen, Peter. 2008. *The Problem of Evil*. Oxford University Press.

Velasquez, Manuel G. 2005. "The Ethics of Consumer Production". *Business Ethics*. Allhoff, Fritz and Vaidya, Anand (eds.). Sage Publications.

Von Clausewitz, Carl, 2012. *On War*. CreateSpace Independent Publishing.

Westacott, Emrys. 2020. "Moral Relativism". *The Internet Encyclopedia of Philosophy*. https://iep.utm.edu/moral-re/

White, Marney. 2018. "Drinking, Smoking, Carousing: Why 'Baby it's Cold Outside' is actually a Feminist Anthem". *USA Today*. https://www.usatoday.com/story/opinion/2018/12/11/baby-its-cold-outside-christmas-song-feminist-anthem-column/2242568002/

Wittmer, Carrie. 2018. "17 Times 'The Simpsons' Accurately Predicted the Future." *Business Insider*. https://www.businessinsider.com/the-simpsons-is-good-at-predicting-the-future-2016-11

Xie, Michael. 2018. "AI Doesn't Eliminate Jobs, it Creates them" *Forbes*. https://www.forbes.com/sites/forbestechcouncil/2018/05/01/ai-doesnt-eliminate-jobs-it-creates-them/#d35581133e70

Yglesias, Matthew. 2016. "How much Credit does Bill Clinton Really Deserve for the 1990s Boom?" *Vox*. https://www.vox.com/2016/4/14/11413352/clinton-economy-credit-90s

Zedpmg. Mao. 1957. *Speech at the Chinese Communist Party's National Conference on Propaganda Work*.

Glossary

Abduction (i.e. abductive arguments) – a form of non-deductive reasoning; arguments "to the best explanation". What counts as best is what is the explanation that is most simple.

Ad Hominem – an informal fallacy; occurs when someone attacks an arguer instead of (or when they should be attacking) an argument.

Addition (Add) – a rule of inference in standard propositional logic which states that if you have a sentence, you may infer a disjunction with that sentence and any other sentence as the disjuncts.

Appeal to Ignorance – an informal fallacy; occurs when someone argues that something must be true simply because it hasn't been or can't be proven false.

Appeal to Inappropriate Authority – an informal fallacy; occurs when someone believes or argues that something is true based on the testimony of a non-expert.

Appeal to Incredulity – an informal fallacy; occurs when one concludes that a claim must be false simply because it *seems* fantastic or defies "common sense".

Appeal to Popularity – an informal fallacy; occurs when it is argued that something is true simply because a large number of people believe it to be true.

Analysis – to give an analysis of something is to study it by breaking it down into its parts.

Antecedent – the part of a conditional that comes directly after the "if". In the formal conditional 'X $\rightarrow$ Y', the antecedent is X.

Argument – a set of ideas that can be divided into premises and a conclusion.

Begging the Question – an informal fallacy; occurs when, in order to make their argument, one assumes the very point at issue. Put differently, their conclusion can be found as one of their assumptions.

Bi-conditional – an "if, and only if" claim. In formal logic, it is (often) represented by a $\leftrightarrow$. A bi-conditional is only true when both components are true, or both components are false.

Components – the parts of a bi-conditional. In the formal bi-conditional 'X ↔ Y', the components are X and Y.

Conclusion – the part of an argument which is an idea or claim inferred from the premises.

Conditional – an "if, then" claim. In formal logic, it is (often) represented by a →. A conditional is only false when the antecedent is true, and the consequent is false.

Conditional Proof (CP) – a rule of inference in standard propositional logic (employing hypothetical reasoning) which states that if – by adding some new assumption – you can derive (i.e. infer) some new sentence, you may infer a conditional with the new assumption as the antecedent and the newly derived sentence as the consequent.

Conjunction (Conj) – a rule of inference in standard propositional logic which states that if you have any two sentences, you may infer a conjunction in which they are the conjuncts.

Conjunction (Operator) – an "and" or a "but" claim. In formal logic, it is (often) represented by a &. A conjunction is only true when both conjuncts are true.

Conjuncts – the parts of a conjunction. In the formal conjunction 'X & Y', the conjuncts are X and Y.

Consequent – the part of a conditional that comes directly after the "then". In the formal conditional 'X → Y', the consequent is Y.

Contradiction – a conjunction of any sentence and its negation.

Deductive Argument – An argument is a deductive argument if and only if, the truth of the premises guarantees the truth of the conclusion. In other words, an argument is a deductive argument if it would be impossible for the premises to be true and the conclusion to be false.

Differentia – a set of distinguishing characteristics.

Disjunction (Operator) – an "Either-or" claim. In formal logic, it is (often) represented by a v. A(n inclusive) disjunction is only false when both disjuncts are false.

Disjunctive Syllogism (DS) – a rule of inference in standard propositional logic which states that if you have a disjunction and the negation of one of the disjuncts, you may infer the other disjunct.

Disjuncts – the parts of a disjunction. In the formal disjunction 'X v Y', the disjuncts are X and Y.

Enthymeme – an argument with at least one premise that is not explicitly stated.

Equivocation – an informal fallacy; occurs when one makes an argument containing the same word multiple times as if it has the same meaning in each instance though it in fact has different meanings.

Exclusive 'or' – a disjunctive claim which is false when both disjuncts are true. For example, if Bill tells Fran "Either I will take *you* to the dance, or I will take Sheila to the dance." Assuming Bill is using an exclusive 'or', and he takes Fran to the dance, *and he takes Sheila to the dance*, what Bill said was false.

Fallacy – a flaw or an error in reasoning.

Fallacy of Composition – an informal fallacy; occurs when one argues that because a member of a group has a certain property, the group as a whole must have that property as well.

Fallacy of Division – an informal fallacy; occurs when one argues that because a particular thing has a certain property, all of its parts must have that property as well.

False dichotomy – an informal fallacy; occurs when one concludes that something is true based on a set of assumptions that erroneously limits the options that are in fact available.

Figurative Language – to use figurative language is to use terms in a way that goes beyond their most typical or basic sense by using metaphor or allegory.

Formal Fallacy – an invalid argument; an argument that is presented as a deductive argument even though it is possible for the premises to be true and the conclusion to be false.

Gambler's Fallacy – an informal fallacy; occurs when one reasons under the assumption that two independent events are somehow causally connected to one another.

Genetic Fallacy – an informal fallacy; occurs when one concludes that something must have a certain property simply because it had that property at its origin.

Genus – a broad category of things.

Hasty Generalization – an informal fallacy; occurs when one makes an inductive inference base on a(n inappropriately) small amount of evidence.

Hypothetical Syllogism (HS) – A rule of inferences in standard propositional logic which states that if you have two conditionals: (i) and (ii), and the consequent of (i) is the same sentence as the antecedent of (ii), you may infer a third conditional with the antecedent of (i) and the consequent of (ii).

Inclusive 'or' – a disjunctive claim which is true when both disjuncts are true. For example, if Bill tells Fran "I will either take you to the dance, or to the movies." Assuming Bill is using an inclusive 'or', and he takes Fran to the dance, *and then he takes Fran to the movies*, what Bill said was still true.

Induction (i.e. inductive arguments) – see: non-deductive arguments.

Informal Fallacy – an error in reasoning that is not an invalid argument but has a common flawed assumption.

Invalid (i.e. Invalidity) – An argument is invalid if and only if it does not follow a proper deductive form (i.e. if it is not a valid argument). So, if an argument is invalid, then if the premises are true, the conclusion may still be false. The truth table for an invalid argument form will be one in which there is at least one row in which all of the premises get a T (in the columns for their main operators), but the conclusion gets an F (in the column for its main operator).

Jointly exhaustive – a categorization is jointly exhaustive if and only if every referent can be placed into at least one species.

Law of Identity – everything is identical with itself; thus, all sentences of the form $P \rightarrow P$ are logically true.

Law of Non-contradiction – no proposition is both true and false. Thus, all sentences of the form P & – P are logically false.

Law of the Excluded Middle – every proposition is either true or false. Thus, all sentences of the form P v – P are logically true.

Literal Language – to use literal language is to use terms in their most typical or basic sense without the use of metaphor or allegory.

Logic – the study of arguments.

Logically Contingent (Pair of Sentences) – A pair of sentences is logically contingent if and only if in a truth table the columns for their main operators are the same in at least one row but not every row.

Logically Contingent (Sentence) – A sentence that is logically contingent is either true or false, not simply because of its logical structure, but because of the facts in the world. In a truth table, the column for the main operator of a logically contingent sentence will contain at least one T and at least one F.

Logically Contradictory – A pair of sentences is logically contradictory if and only if in a truth table the columns for their main operators are exactly the opposite from one another.

Logically Equivalent – A pair of sentences is logically equivalent if and only if in a truth table the columns for their main operators are identical.

Logically False – A sentence that is logically false is false simply because of its logical structure; it will be false no matter how the world is. In a truth table, the column for the main operator of a logically false sentence will be all F's.

Logically True – A sentence is logically true simply because of its logical structure; it will be true no matter how the world is. In a truth table, the column for the main operator of a logically true sentence will be all T's.

Loki's Wager – an informal fallacy; occurs when it is argued that a meaningful conversation or debate cannot be had about a particular concept (or term) without a flawless definition of that concept (or term).

Modus Ponens (MP) – a rule of inference in standard propositional logic which states that if you have a conditional, and the antecedent of that conditional, you may infer the consequent of that conditional.

Modus Tollens (MT) – a rule of inference in standard propositional logic which states that if you have a conditional, and the negation of the consequent of that conditional, you may infer the negation of the antecedent of that conditional.

Mutually exclusive – a categorization is mutually exclusive if and only if no referent can be placed in more than one species.

Naturalistic Fallacy – an informal fallacy; occurs when one argues from purely descriptive premises to a normative (or value-laden) conclusion.

Negation (operator) – a "not" or an "It is not the case that..." claim. In formal logic, it is often represented by a –. A negation is only true when the sentence that is being negated is false (and *vice versa*).

No True Scotsman – an informal fallacy; occurs when one attempts to evade an objection to their universal generalization by excluding a potential counterexample in an *ad hoc* (or seemingly arbitrary) manner.

Non-deductive Argument – An argument is a non-deductive argument if and only if, the truth of the premises only makes the conclusion more likely to be true.

'Or' Elimination (vE) – a rule of inference in standard propositional logic (employing hypothetical reasoning) which states that if you have a disjunction and you can derive a new sentence by assuming both disjuncts (individually), you may infer that new sentence.

Post-Hoc Fallacy – an informal fallacy; occurs when (for any two events: E_1 and E_2) one concludes that E_2 was caused or produced by E_1 simply because it followed E_1.

Premise – the (or a) part of an argument which is supposed to be evidence for or a reason to believe the conclusion.

Principle of Explosion – the idea that if you assume a contradiction, you can prove any sentence; anything follows from a contradiction.

Proposition – the idea expressed by a declarative sentence; an idea that is either true or false.

Red Herring – an informal fallacy; occurs when one diverts attention from the question at hand by raising a related but ultimately irrelevant issue.

Reductio Ad Absurdum (RAA) – a rule of inference in standard propositional logic (employing hypothetical reasoning) which states that if – by adding a new assumption – you can derive a contradiction, you may infer the negation of the newly added assumption.

Referent – in categorization, a particular thing.

Rule of Replacement – a rule of logical inference that is based on logical equivalence which states that if two sentences are logically equivalent, you may infer one from the other (and *vice versa*).

Self-contradiction – A sentence is self-contradictory if and only if it is false simply because of its logical structure; it will be false no matter how the world is. In a truth table, the column for the main operator will be all F's.

Simplification (Simp) – a rule in standard propositional logic which states that if you have a conjunction, you may infer either conjunct.

Semantics – the meaning of our everyday language (or of any sign or symbol whatsoever).

Slippery Slope – an informal fallacy; occurs when one argues – with little or dubious evidence – that a particular inciting event will set off a chain reaction, inevitably resulting in harmful or undesirable consequences.

Sound (i.e. Soundness) – An argument is sound if and only if it is valid and has all true premises.

Species – a narrow category of things; a subcategory of things.

Straw Man – an informal fallacy; occurs when one responds to a distorted or particularly weak caricature of their opponent's argument, as opposed to their opponent's argument itself.

Sunk Cost Fallacy – an informal fallacy; occurs when one makes a cost/benefit calculation about the rationality of some potential future action, but in so doing, factors in a previously invested resources which cannot be recovered.

Syntax – the logical structure of our language without the meaning; the way the semantics of our language is put together.

Tautology – A sentence that is true simply because of its logical operators or structure; it will be true no matter how the world is. In a truth table, the column for the main operator will be all T's.

Truth Conditions – the conditions under which a sentence is either true or false.

Truth Value – the value of a proposition indicating its truth. A true proposition's truth value is True or T; a false proposition's truth value is False or F.

Valid (i.e. Validity) – An argument is valid if and only if it follows a proper deductive form (i.e. if it really is a deductive argument). So, if an argument is valid, if its premises are true, the conclusion must be true. The truth table for a valid argument form will be one in which, in every row in which all the premises get a T (in the columns for their main operators), then the conclusion will get a T as well (in the column for its main operator).

Made in the USA
Monee, IL
02 January 2022

87751485R00178